LIGHT FOR DAYS OF DARKNESS

A DEVOTIONAL OUTLINE
AND
SERMONIC EXPOSITION OF
THE BOOK OF ISAIAH

Ron M. Phillips, D. Min.

D1470509

Evangel Publications
P.O. BOX 11007 / HUNTSVILLE, AL 35814

LIGHT FOR DAYS OF DARKNESS

Copyright © 1996 by

Evangel Ministries, Inc.
Huntsville, Alabama

ISBN: 0-935515-16-X

Scripture quotations in this volume are from the
New King James Version of the Bible.

Published by

EVANGEL PUBLICATIONS
P.O. Box 11007 / Huntsville, Al 35814
(205) 533-5411

Printed in the United States of America

CONTENTS

Contents Continued

PUBLISHER'S PREFACE

EVANGEL PUBLICATIONS is the publishing division of Evangel Ministries, Inc., a non-profit organization. Our purpose is to publish Christian materials that help God's people in their spiritual growth and service to Christ. Our three-fold objective is to: *Exalt the Savior, Evangelize the Sinner,* and *Edify the Saint.*

This is the seventh book we have published for Dr. Ron Phillips. He has done a superb job in providing the materials that meet our objective. I am pleased to bestow special recognition upon him for these messages which are outstanding exposition of the Word of God. They were preached from his own pulpit, televised and distributed internationally through *The Central Message.* I encourage you to call or write for further information and a catalog of other available resources from this ministry:

THE CENTRAL MESSAGE
5208 Hixson Pike / Hixson, Tn 37343
1-(423) 877-6462

Of special interest are two best-selling books:
Home Improvement:
A Maintenance & Repair Manual For Families

Vanquishing The Enemy:
Triumphant In The Battles Of Life

If you are challenged, and helped by the simple presentation of the sermonic exposition of Isaiah, and the other books by Dr. Phillips, to go further in your quest of truth, our goal will be accomplished. May our Lord enable you to that end—and may these messages from Isaiah's prophecy prove to be in your life: *LIGHT FOR DAYS OF DARKNESS.*

- Dr. Sam Wolfe
Editor and Publisher
Huntsville, Alabama

OTHER EVANGEL PUBLICATIONS

By Ron Phillips:

The Royal Law Of Royal Living
(James: A Sermonic Exposition)

God's Call To A Corrupt Nation
(Malachi: A Sermonic Exposition)

Invitation To Intimacy
(Song of Solomon: A Sermonic Exposition)

The Church: Transformed To Triumph
(II Corinthians: A Sermonic Exposition)

The Books: Hebrews and John by Dr. Phillips are out of print.

By Sam Wolfe:

Lessons In Leadership
(Nehemiah: Four reasons why God used him)

Blessed Assurance (New)
(Dealing With Doubt of Salvation)

Building The House Of Prayer (A Study Guide) (New)
(Understanding the Biblical Principles of Prayer)

The Rotation Visitation Program (Revised edition)
(An alternative to the traditional approach)

By J. Mike Minnix:

Panorama Of The Bible (A Study Guide) (New)
(A panoramic view from Genesis to Revelation)

Panorama Of The Bible: Pastor's Supplement (New)

By Jerry Vines:

Jerry Vines' Expository Outlines (The Gospels)

Jerry Vines' Expository Outlines (Acts & Romans)

—◇—

Call or write for information on these and other helps:

Evangel Publications
PO Box 11007, Huntsville, AL 35814
(205) 533-5411

AUTHOR'S PREFACE

Isaiah has been called *the evangelical prophet* because of his clear prophecies of the coming of Christ. In this volume, our purpose is evangelical and typical in approach. I believe, as did our Lord, that there was only one Isaiah. As one who holds to the inerrancy and authority of Scripture, I have written from a conservative perspective. I believe that Isaiah looked ahead and saw Jesus Christ upon the cross and upon the throne. I make no apology for believing that Isaiah's prophecy has a word for the future.

This volume is by no means an exhaustive scholarly exegesis of the book of Isaiah—It is a practical exposition. The messages here are presented with the outline intact. The target audience included the Sunday congregation and a large television and radio audience. Consequently, they are simple, brief, evangelistic and practical.

All of the messages were developed to stand alone conclusively so that those who heard could understand, even if they missed the previous material. The messages are for the people of God and for those whom God is summoning, through Christ, to be His people.

It is my desire that the messages in this volume will be helpful to those who intend to study Isaiah's prophecy more thoroughly.

Dr. Ron M. Phillips
Hixson, Tennessee

INTRODUCTION OF
THE BOOK OF ISAIAH

1. The Prophet:

We know very little about Isaiah's background except the name of his father, Amoz. He seems to have been related to the royal house because of his close relationship to the kings, especially Uzziah. He was called by God, at the death of Uzziah, in a glorious vision in the Temple. He breached protocol and actually entered the Holy of Holies where he had a vision of the Lord being worshiped by angels. After this encounter he gave himself more fully to the work (See Isaiah 6). I believe he was already serving in the office of prophet, but he was transformed and set on fire by the theophany. Tradition says Isaiah was sawn in half by Manasseh.

2. The Period:

Isaiah's ministry stretched historically across the reigns of four monarchs: Uzziah, Jotham, Ahaz and Hezekiah. His ministry, dated variously by scholars, stretched from 758 B.C. possibly to 698 B.C. Some scholars date it from 742 B.C. - 701 B.C. His ministry covered nearly fifty years of the history of Israel.

These years were characterized by four major crises. *One*, the Syro-Ephramitic crisis is covered in Isaiah 7. Syria and Ephraim (Northern Israel) signed a treaty against Judah and its king, Ahaz, who refused to respond in faith. *Two*, the Sennacherib crisis took place when Hezekiah was king. Assyria, under Sennacherib laid siege to Jerusalem. He was thwarted when an angel of God destroyed his army. He died later at the hand of his own family (Isaiah 36-37). *Three*, the next crisis was the near death of Hezekiah and his miraculous healing (Isaiah 38). This gave Hezekiah a chance to have an additional fifteen years of life. During this time he sired the heir to the throne, Manasseh, whom the Bible portrays as the most wicked man in the Old Testament. *Four*, the final crisis was the rise of the Babylonian empire which would result in the captivity of

Judea in 586 B.C. Isaiah prophesied of this captivity and Israel's return. So graphic were these prophecies that some believe a second and even a third Isaiah must have written them. Our Lord quoted from every section of Isaiah's prophecy and cited only one Isaiah.

3. The Purpose:

Isaiah's prophecy included both judgment and redemption. The book falls naturally into two divisions divided by an historical interlude. Isaiah 1-35 is prophetical in the sense of giving warnings of judgment. Isaiah 36-39 is the historical interlude concerning Hezekiah. Isaiah 40-66 is the comfort section. This section contains the wonderful Messianic servant poems that point to the coming of Jesus Christ.

4. The Promise:

Isaiah's ministry included dire warnings to his day. Yet no one can deny the predictive element in his message. The following passages clearly predict Christ:

a. Isaiah 4:2 - Jesus is the branch of the Lord.
b. Isaiah 7:14 - Jesus is the son of the virgin.
c. Isaiah 9:6-7 - Jesus is the child born and the son given on whose shoulders the government rests.
d. Isaiah 11:1 - Jesus is the root of Jesse.
e. Isaiah 28:16 - Jesus is the cornerstone.
f. Isaiah 40:11 - Jesus is the good shepherd.
g. Isaiah 42:1-3 - Jesus is the servant in whom the Lord delights.
h. Isaiah 49:6 - Jesus is the light of the Gentiles.
i. Isaiah 50:6, 53:1-6 - Jesus is the suffering Savior.
j. Isaiah 61:1 - Jesus is the anointed preacher of the gospel. (See Luke 4:18.)
k. Isaiah 63:1-6 - Jesus is the blood-stained conqueror who has tread the wine press alone.
l. Isaiah 66 - Jesus is the Prince of Peace.

As you read Isaiah, you will also discover promises of a millennial age when the world will know peace. Furthermore, this glorious book contains many promises applicable to the individual believer.

The name Isaiah means *Jehovah saves*. The book speaks to every age. Our world faces new crises periodically, yet God still operates providentially. Through faith in the Christ, we can have inward peace now and will have world peace under His reign.

5. The Principles:

Isaiah's theology permeates the entire prophecy. Note these repeated convictions throughout the book:

    a. Sovereignty of God - ch. 6
    b. Holiness of God - ch. 6
    c. Judgment of God - chs. 5, 24, 26
    d. Redemption of God - 41:1-20
    e. Faith in God - 26:3
    f. Coming of the Messiah and His death and resurrection - 7:14, 9:6-9, 53:1-12
    g. Life after death - 26:19
    h. A new earth without war and death - 65:17-25
    i. Israel chastened and restored - ch. 60
    j. Forgiveness of sins - 1:18, 53:6

TEACHING OUTLINE OF ISAIAH

Introduction:

Date: 742-701 B.C.
Author: Isaiah the Prophet
Setting: Jerusalem, during the reigns of Uzziah, Jothom, Ahaz and Hezekiah
Theme: God's redemption of a people for His name.
Main Ideas: 1. Holiness of God - 1:4
              2. Sinfulness of Man - 1:18
              3. Judgment of God - 5:25-26
              4. Faith in God - 7:9
              5. Redemption - ch. 53

I. **The Judgments of a Mighty God** - chs. 1-39

    A. Call and Early Preaching - chs. 1-6
        1. God's Subpoena - ch. 1
            a. Presentation of Charge - 1:2-9
            b. Plea of Defense - 1:10-17
            c. Possibility of Pardon - 1:18-23
            d. Pronouncement of Sentence - 1:24-31
        2. Three Visions of the City of God - chs. 2-4
            a. Vision of the Ideal Jerusalem - 2:1-4
            b. Vision of the Real Jerusalem - 2:5-4:1
            c. Vision of the Purified Jerusalem 4:2-6
        3. Righteous God and Rotten Grapes - ch. 5
            a. Allegory of the Vineyard
            b. Application of the Vineyard
            c. Announcement of Vengeance
        4. Call of God - ch. 6
            a. Confrontation - 6:1-4
            b. Confession - 6:5
            c. Cleansing - 6:6-7
            d. Commission - 6:8-13
    B. Crisis and Promise - chs. 7-12
        1. Birth of Immanuel Foretold - 7:1-17
            a. Historical Occasion - 7:1-9
            b. God's Sign to His People 7:10-16
        2. The Assyrian Invasion Foretold - 7:18-8:15
            a. Ahaz Instructed - 7:18-25
            b. Appeal to the Populace - 8:1-15

Sermon 1

GOD'S COURTROOM
Isaiah 1:1-20

Introduction:

God's prophet had a manifold ministry. First, he had his eye on the course of his nation's history in his own day. Second, he had his hand on the pulse of the spiritual life of God's people. Third, the prophet had his ear attuned to the voice of God. Fourth, the prophet spoke to the needs of his own day. Finally, the prophet looked ahead and declared the place of God's people in the prophetic sweep of future events, giving hope to the righteous and warning to the wicked.

Isaiah was a walking sermon. His name means *Yahweh saves.* He was an aristocrat of the royal house of David. A dramatic vision summoned Isaiah to his divine mission from an affluent lifestyle. Since he was the prophet of the court, he had unrestricted access to all four of the kings who reigned during his forty year ministry. Isaiah had two sons whose names represent the two major themes of the book. We shall meet these boys later.

Isaiah lived in difficult days. Nations were moving to war. Empires were crumbling and new ones rising to prominence. Israel and Judah were perched between the world powers, Egypt and Assyria. Spiritual life in the nation was in decline. Although religion was at an all time high, there was not much righteousness.

Isaiah's opening message summoned the nation to court —not the court of human jurisprudence, but the court of divine justice! This divine arraignment had both Heaven and earth for its audience. There was a threefold word from the Lord to the people:

I. The Divine Indictment (1:2-10)

Isaiah made it very clear that it was God who was both judge and prosecuting attorney. What Isaiah said came

15

from what he had seen in the vision from God (1:1). This message was what "the Lord hath spoken" (1:2). This indictment was not less than "the word of the Lord" (1:10). Isaiah was the human instrument but they were to understand that "the mouth of the Lord hath spoken it" (1:20).

The indictment had the tone of amazement and astonishment, for the people had sinned against the goodness of God. Their sin is more horrible as it is seen in contrast to the five-fold description of God as: *Father, Lord, Leader, Doctor, Protector.*

1. Rebelled Against Their Father (1:2)

God is a loving Father who has reared and provided for His own. This was true of the nation Israel. God had brought them out of paganism to a special land and had provided wonderfully for them. Then they "rebelled," which means *to fall away from and to rise up against.* God's children had both fallen from their high calling and, if that were not bad enough, they had stood up with a fist in the face of their Father.

2. Forsook Their Lord (1:3-4)

God is not only Father—He is Lord and owner. Ignorant animals will go to the owner's crib for feeding. These people had quit feeding at the Father's table and had gone after the husks of the world.

3. Turned Their Backs on Their Leader (1:4b)

Here God is characterized as the Holy One of Israel, Isaiah's favorite designation. He is their leader and yet they turned their backs and refused to go where God was leading.

4. Refused the Cure of Their Doctor (1:5-6)

Because of their sin, they had been chastened by disease. They were a sick nation, and yet they refused to let God close their wounds or pour the oil of the Holy Spirit upon their sores.

5. Forgot Their Protector (1:7-9)

The nation was not only diseased—it was also "desolate." This is a description of a nation that has lost the protection of God. He is the "Lord of hosts." This speaks of his majestic authority over the armies of Heaven. He had only a small remnant that kept His protection over the nation.

Look at our nation today! Verse 4 says "Alas, sinful

nation." This could be rendered *shame*. We have forsaken God. Our nation is sick. We have turned our backs on His Word and leadership. Only a small remnant keeps God's wrath off this nation today.

II. **The Divine Instruction** (1:10-15)

Israel's sin was not to be understood by the externals. They gave, they attended, and they prayed. It is as if they have answered the charges with their defense. "Look, Isaiah, we give large sacrifices. We attend all the special services. We raise our hands and pray. What more does God expect?"

God's instruction was Biblical. Look at Sodom and Gomorrah! Ezekiel 16:49-50 summarizes the sins of Sodom: "pride, fullness of bread, abundance of idleness, neither did she strengthen the hand of the poor and needy and they were proud and committed abomination before me..."

Sin was tolerated, the needy neglected, and the people of God were comfortable. Yet God said to them "your hands are full of blood." Why? They had not reached their own people with God's word!

Oh, beloved, we dare not allow ourselves to become formalists. We dare not gather in pride and forget our lost and needy neighbors. The poorest man or woman in this city is the one who is lost without Jesus.

III. **The Divine Invitation** (1:15-18)

Notice three wonderful truths about God's invitation:

1. It Is Gracious.

When you read this catalog of failure and then hear the voice of God saying in spite of it, "Come," it stirs the soul. We can come to God because Jesus has come to us. In Psalm 40:7 the Lord says, "Lo, I come to do thy will, O my God." Because He has come, we can now hear His voice inviting us to come.

2. It Is Simple.

He calls for reason on the part of God's people. They can see that God graciously offers them the care of a Father, the healing of a physician, the protection of an army, and the salvation of the Lord. It is not complicated. All you must do is heed His call to "come" willingly and obediently.

3. It Is Necessary.

The phrase "your sins be as scarlet" indicates an irreversible condition. Scarlet and crimson represent blood stains on wool which could not be taken out. The dye they used came from an insect, the larvae of a cochineal beetle. Once dyed, the white material could never be white again.

That is the condition of a sinner. We can do nothing about sin. We are stained permanently with our sin until we come to Christ. He can take our sins away. His crimson blood can take our scarlet, sin-stained souls and make them white as snow.

4. It Is Urgent.

God says, "Come now!" There is no time to waste. This is the time of God's gracious call. We dare not say to God, "Not now." Karl Menninger, the noted psychiatrist once said, "If I could convince people that their sins are forgiven, seventy-five percent could leave the mental wards whole!"

Conclusion:

A little boy was watching the red-coated British soldiers march in a parade in London. He said, "Father, look at the soldiers dressed in white." His dad argued, "Son, they have on red." The boy responded, "No, dad, they are all dressed in white." The father looked down and saw that the bottom of the window was tinted red. When you look at red through red, it appears white. When our Lord looks at our sin stained soul, He looks through the blood of Jesus and we are white as snow.

Here is an indictment and an invitation. Christians have the scarlet stains of bloody hands, the lives of those with whom we have not shared Jesus. God calls us to court. Let us be clean today and from now on. God calls the hell bound sinner to court. And He promises, "You can be as white as snow."

— ✧ —

OUR CITY AND GOD'S CITY
Isaiah 1:21-4:6

Introduction:

The cities of America are in serious trouble. This is most evident in the capitol city of our nation, Washington, D.C. The government of that city is described as the most inept in America.

Washington has more police officers per citizen than any other city in the U.S., yet the crime rate continues to rise every year. The number of murders is especially high, making the city of Washington the murder capitol of America.

Washington spends six thousand dollars per pupil per year in the schools, yet the school system has a forty-four percent drop out rate. Very few members of Congress send their children to the public schools.

For every twenty thousand loans processed for renewing housing, it costs eleven thousand dollars. There is one city employee for every thirteen citizens in D.C. Drugs, rape, murder, pornography, thievery, and prostitution are prevalent problems that characterize our national city.

Washington is a picture of the cities of our nation. With vast resources available, we face the worst problems imaginable.

Isaiah lived in such a city. He was a man of the city. God had set forth an ideal for His city, Jerusalem. However, the city was marked by the same problems we face today. Please give consideration to these thoughts found in these Scriptures:

I.   **The Corrupt City** (1:21-23, 2:15-11)

1.   Corrupt Leadership (1:21-23)
A nation will have rules that reflect their own standards. We get what we deserve in leadership.

    2.   Corrupt Religion (2:5-6)
Eastern religion with its false philosophy has taken over the politics and the entertainment industry.
    3.   Corrupt Values (2:7-9)
A nation makes idols out of things and worships the work of its own hands.

II. **The Condemned City** (2:12-4:1)

How can you tell when you are in a city or society that is under judgment?
    1.   Pride in Human Achievement (2:12-22)
Everything accomplished in this city was to man's glory.
    2.   Loss of Material Gain (3:1)
The necessities of life will become scarce.
    3.   Loss of Manliness and Courage (3:2-3)
The nation will allow itself to be passed around by other nations.
    4.   Society Controlled by Unruly Youth and Ungodly Women (3:4-27).

This description speaks of our modern society that exalts youth and women's rights. Phyllis Schafly recently spoke of a woman being named as head cadet at West Point. "Our enemies must tremble" she said.
    5.   Wars that Take the Lives of the Young Men (3:25-4:1).

War is God's judgment on a nation and world. Nations that disregard God will face war.
    6.   Ultimate Judgment of the Great Tribulation.
Isaiah 2:12 speaks of the "day of the Lord." This is the day of God's judgment on the godless society man has built upon this earth. Isaiah 2:21 speaks of the "terror of the Lord" when He comes in judgment. In Revelation 18, the city of Babylon represents the city of man. In Revelation 18:13-16 we read the catalog of merchandise. Notice that the city trafficked in the bodies and souls of human beings. Ultimately, God will judge our society because of its disregard for the value of human life.

Isaiah 3:9 speaks of "Sodom" (See Isaiah 1:9, Ezekiel 16:49). Remember, that city faced the awesome destruction by God. Already we see the evidence of approaching judgment on our society.

III. **The Coming City** (2:1-4, 4:2-6)

Certainly, revival can change a city for a period of time. Ultimately, we must "flee the city." This does not mean to leave literally, but to be careful to remember that much of our society and city is temporary. Let us be careful not to be caught up in the sins of the city.

Indeed the church is to be a "city set on a hill" with the light of the gospel. In the Old Testament God gave "cities of refuge" for fugitives to flee to when in danger. The church is the *city of refuge* for those who are tired of the *city of man*.

Yet the vision of Isaiah stretched beyond to a coming city. It will be the city of God. G. Campbell Morgan said of that city, "It will be marked by material prosperity, moral purity, and mighty protection" (4:2-6). And I would add that it will be a city of peace (2:1-4).

Indeed the city of God will be God's city. Hebrews 12:22-24 speaks of the believer coming to that glorious city. When we die, then we come to the city.

Yet, one of these days that city is coming down to the earth for the glorious reign of God over the earth. Revelation 21:2-8 speaks of that glorious city of God.

Conclusion:

Hebrews 11:10 speaks of Abraham "waiting" for the city of God. Abraham was never satisfied with man's city; he was looking for God's city.

> Lo heavenly scene, before me rise,
>   The city of our God,
> Its glorious beauties gladden my eyes,
>   Of saints the blessed abode.
>
> See how its pearly gates unfold,
>   To all the ransomed throng,
> When shall I tread its streets of gold,
>   And swell its joyous song.

And there the throne of God I see,
 And there the glorious Lamb,
Who shed His precious blood for me,
 And sin and death o'er came.

Hosannah to the Lamb of God,
 To Thee is glory due.
Oh for a place in Thine abode,
 With saints and angels too.

- Author Unknown

— ✧ —

Sermon 3

GOD'S HOLY HEDGE
Isaiah 5:1-7

Introduction:

One of the prophetic methods that Isaiah used was the *inspired ballad*. Here Isaiah sings this stern message. More than likely, this song was used at some sort of festival where the prophet had been asked to sing.

You can imagine the shock when this special music was heard. It is unusual for Isaiah to use a term such as "beloved" to refer to God whom He called the "Holy One of Israel." However, just as a newly married couple would do anything for each other, a young Isaiah would sing this song for the God he loved.

The content of the song uses familiar scenes that all could understand. In Israel, preparing a field for a vineyard is tedious, costly labor. Israel's soil is fertile but very rocky. The opening of the song speaks of the selection of a site, "a very fruitful hill." This site is fenced and cleared. A watch tower is built. All that is necessary to process the fruit into wine is provided, but the field yields rotten grapes.

The owner and master of the vineyard pronounces judgment. His judgment is to remove the two-fold hedge and wall, and allow it to be laid waste. Isaiah 5:5 sums up the awful judgment of God, which is abandoning a nation to its own devices.

I am convinced that God's *hedge* can be placed around a nation, a family, a church, or an individual. I am further convinced that the removal of that *hedge*, next to being sent to hell, is the worst possible judgment. Here we see clearly: the *reality*, the *realms* and the *removal* of God's hedge.

I. The Reality of God's Hedge

In Israel, two walls were constructed around a vineyard. The first was a stone wall, and the second was a hedge of thorns. These walls were designed to keep out

23

both man and beasts. In these Scriptures, the hedge declares five truths we should note:

1. Proprietor of the vineyard (5:1)
God planted the vineyard on His hill. We need to learn that "the earth is the Lord's and the fullness thereof." All nations belong to God. He said "all souls are mine," thus, every family and individual belongs to Him. In Matthew 16:18, He said of the church, "I will build my church." Everything belongs to Him.

2. Preparation of the vineyard (5:2)
God declares that He has made every possible provision necessary for the vineyard to produce. We are not to blame God for the failures caused by our poor stewardship of his provision.

3. Protection of the vineyard (5:2)
God provides a *hedge* around that which is His. Standing above the hedge is a watchman on the tower in the midst of the field. Nothing, absolutely nothing, can get around God's hedge without God's permission.

4. Possibilities of the vineyard (5:2)
God expected good fruit, but He received "wild grapes." That is literally *stinking grapes*. God expects good fruit in His vineyard. Whatever God sets up has the potential of abundant blessing.

5. Privilege of the vineyard (5:2)
In the middle of the vineyard, was a winepress. Wine is always a symbol of joy in scripture (See Proverbs 3:5-10). Life inside the hedge is the life of joy and abundance. It is a foretaste of heaven.

The *hedge* is a reality that we need to *accept* and *appropriate*.

II. **The Realms God Protects with A Hedge**

There are four realms that God protects with the hedge:
1. Nations can enjoy the protection of the hedge.
Isaiah 5 indicates that Israel had experienced and enjoyed that privilege. Our America had a *hedge* in its early days. America's victory over Britain was a miracle. The Great Awakening and the fire of God in the churches placed that

hedge. Nations can enjoy divine blessings.

2. Families can live behind the hedge.

Job 1:1-10 indicates that Job, by prayer and sacrifice, kept a hedge of protection around his family. In the same way, believing parents can erect a prayer hedge around their families.

3. Individuals can be hedged in with God.

In Hosea 2, the prophet's sinning wife is hedged up by the prayers of the prophet. She persisted in trying to break out until she was broken by her actions and came home to Hosea. Prayer hedges can be built around individuals.

4. Churches need the hedge of protection.

Churches need to be protected and the hedge needs to be built and repaired regularly.

III. The Removal of the Hedge

In Isaiah 5:5, God judges His vineyard by removing the hedge of protection. This makes the vineyard accessible to those who would steal and pillage. Every beast of the field would have access to the vineyard.

God's most terrifying judgment on this earth is abandonment to evil. When God removes His hedge, destructive agents and influences are free to operate in that unprotected realm. This is true of nations, families, individuals and churches. *Why does God remove the hedge?*

1. In rare cases, God removes the hedge to prove His servant and to prove Satan a liar. This is true in the cases of Joseph and Job. Both of them battled the enemy and gained the victory. When God purposes to accomplish His objectives in the lives of His own, He will show up in power and Satan will be exposed and defeated.

2. God removes the hedge when His order of authority is violated. First, when one in authority fails to fulfill God-given responsibilities, the hedge is broken down. Wicked and ungodly leadership will cause the removal the hedge from a nation.

Second, when pastoral authority is forfeited by moral failure, the church is infiltrated by evil. Also, when pastoral authority is resisted or removed without good cause, a church loses its hedge.

Third, when a father does not stand in the gap for his children and wife, then evil will have access to his family. What you think and do in secret that is displeasing to God opens up your family to demonic attack.

3.   Moral failure will remove the hedge.

Isaiah 5 lists the sins that cause God to remove the hedge. A moral confusion will open the door to every kind of wicked attack.

    a.   Alcohol becomes a national disgrace (5:11, 22).

    b.   Obsession with entertainment (5:12)

    c.   Moral failure becomes popular (5:18)

    d.   Moral confusion (5:20)

    e.   Self sufficiency (5:2)

4.   Spiritual laziness brings down the hedge (Proverbs 24:30-34). When one is not diligent in spiritual responsibilities, his vineyard will be spoiled.

5.   When the hedge is down, hell enlarges itself (5:14). It dooms the souls of many who are destroyed by the onslaught of the enemy.

IV.   The Rebuilding of the Hedge

1.   God uses prayer (Ephesians 6:10-17).

Believers in full armor can pray.

2.   God uses men faithful to the Word of God to make up the hedge. Note Ezekiel 13:5, 22:30. God was looking for such a man to stand in the gap.

3.   God uses His people to spare the land.

Had ten righteous people been found, Sodom would have been spared.

4.   God uses holy angels to stand in the hedge.

Psalm 34:7 says, "The angel of the Lord encamps around those that fear Him."

5.   Revival rebuilds the hedge (Psalm 80:1-19).

This Psalm is a call to revival. Repentance restores the hedge. Zechariah 1:5 says, "For I, saith the Lord, will be a wall of fire round about, and will be the glory in the midst of her."

6.   Jesus Christ is the rejected stone.

In Mark 12:1-12, Jesus tells the parable of the vineyard. In verse 11, the awful truth is stated, "The "stone" is rejected. Jesus Christ must be the One who is the center of life.

Conclusion:

In those days, there were three walls used to protect the vineyard. At certain seasons an outer wall of *fire* was set to keep predators out of the field. Inside that wall a *thorny hedge* was built which was permanent. The inner wall was a *stone* wall.

My friend, we can have this threefold protection around our nation, our church and our homes: the fire of revival, the hedge of prayer and the Word of God—the chief cornerstone Himself.

We must learn to pray. We must pray at least one hour a day. God would have spared Sodom if one tenth of one percent of the population had been right with God. Someone said that, for our nation, that means three hundred thousand people willing to engage in prayer on a regular basis.

It seems that the church today will do anything but pray. I challenge and encourage you. Bind yourself to God for one hour a day for family, nation, church and self. Then watch God build the hedge and drive out the enemy.

— ✧ —

IT HAPPENED IN CHURCH
Isaiah 6:1-8

Introduction:

Why should anyone attend church? There are so many other things that you could do. One ought to attend faithfully and regularly because the Bible commands it (Hebrews 10:25). One ought to attend faithfully because Jesus blesses it (Hebrews 10:21). One ought to attend faithfully because it encourages others who attend. One ought to attend because there is no other place, like the church, where personal needs can be met in God's way.

Isaiah was a busy and important man. Times were perilous indeed. The king had died and God seemed very far away. When his world caved in, Isaiah went to the Temple. He opened his heart to God and there at the place of worship God met his needs. It happened in church! It happens every Lord's day in one of our services. All may not see God, but someone every Lord's day has needs met and miracles wrought. In these troublesome times, we all need the church. Notice two questions about Isaiah's trip to church.

I.   **What He Took with Him to Church**

1.   A Broken Heart
His king was dead. His leader was gone. He went to church to weep and bring his sorrows before God.

I remember Larry when he came to church. He was dressed in old clothes. He had a little girl with him. She was dressed nicely. At the invitation, he came to the altar. He wept and cried. His wife had abandoned him and the little girl. She became a strip dancer in a club. This young man was heartbroken. When he saw our church building, he came in. He was saved, and God healed his broken heart.

29

You may have a broken heart today. Someone may have hurt you. You may have sorrows no one knows but you. God can touch your spirit today.

2. Shattered Hopes

Isaiah was depending on Uzziah to bring about spiritual awakening. All of his dreams and hopes for his nation were lying in the coffin with Uzziah. He saw no hope for the future. It is a hopeless time for many today. Perhaps marital problems, job problems, family problems or other disappointments have caused it. There are some in this building today who have shattered hopes. This uncertainty about the future drives many to suicide.

3. Guilty Conscience

Isaiah cries out, "I am a man of unclean lips." He brought a heart laden with guilt. He had sinned against the Lord and was weighed down with the burden.

Perhaps you have come today with guilt hanging like a dark cloud over your life. Sins of past and present haunt you. Try as you may—you can't shake off your guilt.

4. Burden for His World

He saw that the whole world was like himself. He saw the sin and uncleanness of the world. It seemed that sin would smother the world. Evil seemed triumphant all around him. He desired to see his world changed, but did not know how to change it. What a mess his world was in!

Our's is no different. Sin abounds. Evil gets rich in temporary treasure. Things wax worse and worse. What can we do for our world?

5. A Need for God

Isaiah desperately needed a touch from God. He was God's prophet, but God seemed very far away. He needed revival.

Isaiah went to church with a broken heart, shattered hopes, sinful conscience and a burden for his world. Thank God, he didn't leave the same way he had gone.

II. What He Left Church With

Something wonderful happened to Isaiah at church. He met God there. He found all of His needs met in Him. When the prophet left church, he left with:

1. A New Perception of God

While in the Temple he had a vision of God. He saw God as King. The throne on earth was empty, but the throne in Heaven is never empty. Uzziah was dead but the Lord was alive and reigning. His hands were still on the reigns of the earth.

Isaiah saw God in His *glory*. The cloud of smoke symbolizes His glory. He saw God in His *holiness*, and heard the angels cry "holy." He saw God in His *mercy*. The throne of glory is also the throne of grace. The Lord sits on the mercy seat. He realized that God was very near indeed. He left with a new perception of God.

2. A New Purity

A coal was brought from the altar of sacrifice and placed upon Isaiah's sinful lips. From the altar came the fire of cleansing and forgiveness. You, too, can leave with a cleansed heart. The blood of Jesus has fueled the flame of forgiveness. God takes away our sins. It matters not how big or how bad the sin. Forgiveness can be yours through Christ. At church is a good place to have your sins forgiven.

3. A New Purpose

Things in the world were bad, but Isaiah discovered that God had not forsaken the world. He found that God is at work through His people in the world. God cries out, "Whom can I send, who will go for us?" Isaiah answers, "Here am I Lord, send me!" He leaves with a new found purpose. He has met God and now he must share what he knows. His reason for living is God. His hope is in God.

Conclusion:

Why do you go to church? You can go to take your burdens and lay them upon the Lord. You don't have to leave untouched and unchanged. What happened to Isaiah happened in church. It can happen to you. Bring your burdens to Christ today.

— ✧ —

THE KING IMMANUEL
Isaiah 7:1-14

Introduction:

735 B.C. was a year of political uncertainty for the ancient world. The nation of Judah was in a state of unrest and confusion. Ambassadors were scurrying to and fro across the middle east signing treaties and making alliances with the awful specter of war and invasion hanging over their heads.

Ahaz was king of Judah, the Southern Kingdom, and was a very disturbed man. Pekah, King of Israel, and Rezin, the king of Syria, had become allies in order to stand against Assyria which was becoming strong under Tiglath-Pileser. Furthermore, this alliance had threatened to invade Judah and Jerusalem because of Ahaz's refusal to join the alliance.

Behind the scenes, we find that God was displeased with Judah before Ahaz came to the throne. While Jotham served the Lord he allowed the pagan places of worship to stand. In judgment, God sent these two kings, Pekah and Rezin against Judah to stir her to faith in Himself. When Jotham died and Ahaz became king, Pekah had been on the throne seventeen years while Ahaz was but a twenty year old youth. In his inexperience, fearfulness and faithlessness, he erred in his estimation of the strength of this enemy.

While the young king is inspecting the water supply, he is confronted by the statesman-prophet, Isaiah, with his young son, Shear-Jashub (a remnant shall return). He delivers to the king the message God has put upon his heart. In verses 4-7, Isaiah gives a four point sermon:

1. Be careful - This is a call to Ahaz not to act hastily or foolishly.

2. Be calm - Don't make an anxious appraisal. Look

33

your enemy in the face and evaluate the threat. Isaiah says correctly, "They are but two stumps about to go out."

3. Be confident - in God's word (vs. 7). It shall not stand, neither shall it come to pass." God says,"believe my word and trust me."

Ahaz's response was a sickly, cowardly self-serving response. He was a forerunner to the modern politician who thinks that governments are above the control of God.

Ahaz rejects the word of God in all his actions. Notice how hastily he sells his God and country into the hands of an enemy. Notice that he passed his little baby son through the fire to false Gods. He sent an ambassador to bribe Tiglath into an alliance. Isaiah said, "the razor you hired will shave you." It would only be a few years before Tiglath's grandson, Sennacherib, would almost overthrow Judah, but for a miraculous intervention of God.

Isaiah confronts this fearful king (vs. 9) and calls him to faith.

-If you will not believe, you shall not last.
-If you have no faith, you shall not stay.
-If your faith is not sure, your throne is not secure.
-If you cannot confide, you will not abide.

David's throne is for a man of faith. Ahaz refused to believe God. He was offered a sign and piously asserted that he did not tempt God. He can sacrifice his son to the harvest goddess, Asherah, and worship on every high hill, but insults the God of all creation by refusing His offer.

Isaiah had the message for Ahaz and Judah, and it is the message for the world today. In Isaiah 7:14, God gives a sign. The sign says three things to Ahaz and to us:

1. You are finished. Though he would reign seventeen years, he would never be remembered as David's son.

2. Your kind of kingdom is finished.

3. A new king and a new kind of kingdom is coming.

The virgin is going to give birth to a Son and He will be Immanuel — God is with us. Yes, in the midst of a crisis-torn world, God is with us. *Jesus is God with us:*

I. Reigning over Us

A new Kingdom is already here. It is the Kingdom of God. His Kingdom is His sovereign rule in the world. At present, this mighty Kingdom is invisible; it has no representatives in the parliaments and councils of this world.

It is called the Kingdom of Heaven and the Kingdom of God. It is a Kingdom of Good News (Matthew 9:35, Luke 8:1). It is an everlasting Kingdom (II Peter 1:11). God's invisible rule will become visible at his appearing. Our assurance in the crises of this world is, God is with us— *reigning*.

II. Revealing Himself to Us

When Jesus was born, the veil was lifted and God was with us revealing Himself to us. Man had longed to know what God is like through the generations. When Jesus came, God's nature was perfectly displayed in all His words and actions.

(Christmas is not man seeking God. It is God seeking man. It is God making known His life to us. He does not promise to take away all burdens or battles, but to give us God's presence in the midst of them. He reveals the resources of God to us.)

The word was made flesh and man beheld His glory, full of grace and truth. Three words describe Him:

1. Glory - God's sinlessness and sovereignty.
2. Grace - God's favor displayed to sinners.
3. Truth - God's word made flesh among us.

III. Redeeming Us to Himself

Jesus came not only to reign and to reveal, He came to redeem. Man's greatest and foremost need is redemption. Nothing else can substitute for the atoning death of Christ on the cross and set him free from the power and penalty of sin. He is a lost sinner until Christ comes into his life to save him. Ahaz needed to trust God for salvation. Men in our day need to trust Him for His redemption. Jesus came to set us free. His *incarnation is humanity's emancipation*.

IV. **Receiving Us to Himself**

The prophet's appeal was for Ahaz to believe God. That is forever the appeal of heaven to our souls! As Abraham considered the dead womb of his wife and the promises of God, man is called to faith in God.

As Moses walks away from Pharaoh's throne to Jethro's tent, he is called to faith.

As Noah built a boat where there was no water and on a planet where before there had been no rain, he is called to faith.

When the disciples laid down their professions and followed Jesus, they were answering by faith. When Paul forsook family and religion for Christ, it was by faith.

The call of Christmas is a call to faith. It is a call to believe the incredible! God came to us in Christ and will receive all who will believe!

"To as many as would receive Him, to them He gave the right to be the sons of God, even to them that believe upon His name" (John 1:12).

Conclusion:

We have two trees in our house. In the den, we have an *old fashion tree* that is decorated with the old stuff—memories of a lifetime.

In the living room, we have our *praise tree* decorated with musical instruments and songs. It towers above the olive wood manger scene on the coffee table. That tree symbolizes the cross of our Savior as the reason for His birth. The tree has no dead Christ, only praise to the living Christ. Will you believe?

— ✧ —

Sermon 6

THE KING REJECTED
Isaiah 8:1-22

Introduction:

In the year 1829, a Philadelphia man named George Wilson robbed the U.S. mails, killing someone in the process. Wilson was arrested, brought to trial, found guilty and sentenced to be hanged. Some friends intervened in his behalf and were finally able to obtain a pardon for him from President Andrew Jackson. When Wilson was informed, he refused to accept the pardon!

The sheriff was unwilling to exact the sentence since the president had pardoned Wilson. An appeal was made to President Jackson who in turn asked the Supreme Court for a ruling. Chief Justice Marshall ruled that a pardon is a piece of paper, the value of which depends on its acceptance by the person implicated. If it is refused, then it is not a pardon. George Wilson was hanged, although a pardon lay on the sheriff's desk.

So it is with God's offer of salvation in Christ. The consequences of refusing are devastating. Unless salvation is received, it is not valid.

God had offered life to Israel. His requirement was faith in His word and submission to His kingship. Ahaz had refused God's offer. He had chosen rather to put his trust in human alliances. In just a few short years, Syria and Israel would be destroyed and the people taken captive. The Assyrian army would besiege Jerusalem (8:1-4). Assyria, like the raging Euphrates River at floodtide, would roll over the nation (8:7-8). The people would be broken—their foolish counsel having failed (8:9-10).

Human alliances and counsel having failed, the people would turn to the occult (8:19). This would leave them in utter darkness. The nation would reject God's offer of pardon for these substitutes for faith.

The world has not changed. Human alliances and

37

treaties are seen as the hope of the world. Human opinion and counsel are elevated above the Word of God. New age religion with its new names for the old occult welcomes many seekers who walk into the dark unknown of cultic religion.

With the problems around us, we personally believe that our contacts and wisdom can get us through. We value the word of experts as that of God. The occult is growing rapidly to offer a religion to a world that has rejected Christ.

Woven into the warnings of Isaiah 8 is a call to those who reject the Lord. What happens to people when the Lord is rejected?

I. **They Miss the Peace of God** (8:6).

The people are indicted for refusing the waters of Shiloah. This was a small peaceful stream that flowed in the environs of Jerusalem. Later, it was channeled into the city and became the pool of Shiloah, or, as it is called in the New Testament, the pool of Siloam.

This gentle stream was called Shiloah because of its peacefulness. The name comes from the same root word as the Hebrew Shalom which means *peace*. The name *Shiloah* is also a derivative of that word. Shiloah is a synonym for the Messiah. In Genesis 49:10, we read, "the scepter shall not depart from Judah, nor a lawgiver from between his feet until Shiloah comes; and to Him shall be the obedience of the people."

Isaiah 9:10 describes our Lord as the "Prince of Peace." The message of the angels at Jesus' birth was "peace on earth." Jesus Christ, God in the flesh, was peace on earth. The earth will never know complete peace until He reigns as King on this earth.

God wants your life to be lived in the waters of Shiloah, our Savior. He is the water of life. He alone can give peace.

I saw a painting once entitled *PEACE*. It was a raging surf crashing on the shore. In one corner of the picture there was a bird asleep in the cleft of the craggy cliff. Jesus is your Shiloah—your peace.

II. **They Ignore the Presence of God** (8:8-10)

I believe all of chapters 7-9 are the *Immanuel* chapters. In Isaiah 7:14, the promised Messiah would be called "Immanuel," which means "God with us." In Isaiah 8:8, the land belongs to Immanuel. In Isaiah 8:10, the nation is warned not to trust their own counsel, but to look to the fact that God is with us.

It is sad that they refused to believe in the presence of God in their lives. He had not come in the flesh, but He was there.

It is even sadder that we who live 2000 years after His coming reject or ignore His presence. Jesus is not *out there*. He has come to be Immanuel— "God with us."

III. **They Forfeit the Protection of God** (8:11-15)

In these verses, God's Messiah is described as a great "Rock." One can find sanctuary in the cleft of the rock and protection in the shadow of the rock. The Lord Jesus is the *Rock of ages*. Two great old hymns emphasize this truth:

> Rock of Ages, cleft for me,
>> Let me hide myself in Thee;
> Let the water and the blood,
>> From Thy wounded side which flowed,
> Be for sin the double cure,
>> Save from wrath and make me pure.
>
> - Toplady

> Beneath the cross of Jesus
>> I fain would take my stand,
> The shadow of a mighty Rock
>> Within a weary land;
> A home within the wilderness,
>> A rest upon the way,
> From the burning of the noontide heat,
>> And the burden of the day.
>
> - St. Christopher

Isaiah then warns that this same Rock, when rejected, becomes a "stone of stumbling and a rock of offense." Paul cites this very passage in Romans 9:1-15. Peter cites this passage in I Peter 2:8. You will either trust Jesus or trip over Jesus. You will either *believe* or be *broken*.

IV. **They Forego the Promises of God** (8:16-20).

In verses 16-18, believers are called to wait on the Lord and put our hope in Him. We are not to look to anything else but His Word (vs. 20). Only the Word of God can give light to the believer.

In verse 18, we read this remarkable statement of Isaiah. This statement is Messianic. Hebrews 2:13 cites it as a prophecy of the coming of Jesus. In other words, Isaiah and his two sons represent what God's Word has promised to the people. He and his two sons are a picture of the hope for which Israel and the world waited.

Remember Isaiah's name means *Jehovah saves*. *Maher-shalal-has-baz* means *spoil speeds, prey hastens or judgment is coming*. *Shear-jashub* means *a remnant will return*. Isaiah and his boys were a walking message. Little *judgment* and *hope* walked on each side of Isaiah. The message is the Messiah is coming. He will be either your *judgment* or your *hope*.

Conclusion:

When Jesus came into the world that first Christmas, Isaiah's prophecy was clearly fulfilled. Yet He met rejection. There was no room for Him in the inn. His own town's people sought to stone Him. The government sought to kill Him. "He came to His own and His own received Him not."

The choice is yours. He will be your *river of life or flood of judgment*. He will be your rock of protection or crushing stone of judgment. He is your greatest *hope* or greatest *dread*. Open your heart to Him.

— ✧ —

Sermon 7

THE KING'S SHOULDERS
Isaiah 9:1-7

Introduction:

The nation that rejects God's Word rejects the light, and is doomed to darkness. Thus, it was with Israel and Judah. Tiglath-Pileser would oppress Israel and later Sargon, the Second of Assyria, would overthrow the Northern Kingdom. Judah would survive another century, though in great difficulty.

Isaiah's prophecy of gloom and darkness came true in Israel. The principle still applies today. The further one steps away from God the darker the night.

This remarkable prophecy is filled with hope. There is hope for the Northern Kingdom called here, Galilee. Indeed, there is hope for the world in the coming of the Messiah. His coming is the hope of all who live in darkness of this age.

The condition of those in darkness is described under three metaphors:

1. Yoke of His burden
A yoke was a tool that harnessed two animals together to pull a load. This describes the people who are away from God. They are yoked to a burden they cannot manage.
2. Staff of His shoulder
This staff was used by a shepherd to keep sheep in line. Here it is a reference to wrong leadership that has taken away freedom.
3. Rod of His oppressor
This was the instrument used to beat animals or people who were out of line.

Israel carried a heavy burden on its shoulder. Their enemies were upon them. These metaphors illustrate the condition of a person in darkness today. *One*, they carry the yoke of the burden of sin. *Two*, they are under the cruel tyranny of the staff of the flesh. *Three,* they are under the oppressive rod of Satan.

The hope of Israel is the hope of the world, and the hope of every human being. God has broken the yoke, the staff and the rod that burdens humanity. How did God do that for us? Let us look in three directions:

I. **Look at the Cradle**.

"For unto us a child is born." The One who would defeat the enemies of the human race was to be a child. The incarnation of Christ was the fulfillment of this promise.

Seven hundred years later in a stable a cry of birth was heard. The labor pains of Mary echo the groaning of a world in darkness. A star lit up the night, signifying the end of darkness for all who would believe. Miracle of miracles, God in a manger-cradle! The glory of God was upon His shoulders.

II. **Look at the Cross**.

"A Son is given." It is one thing for a child to be born; it is quite another to give one's son. You will remember the sadness a few Christmases ago when some of our soldier boys were coming home to a Tennessee Christmas at Clarksville. Those boys died in a plane crash. Those parents had given their sons. In 1988, just four days before Christmas, two hundred Americans were blown out of the sky by terrorists. Most of them were students, children dying on the altar of fanatical terrorism. The outraged parents will never fully recover. None of us would willingly give up a child.

Yet, God the Father sent His Son into this world. Jesus Christ suffered at the hands of the ultimate terrorist, Satan. He was God's gift of grace. Jesus said, "No man takes my life from me, I lay it down willingly."

You see, the shoulders that had carried the ensign of God's glory, had to bear the cross.

III. **Look at the Crown.**

"And the government shall be upon His shoulders." The story does not end with the cradle and the cross. For this "son given," would rise to be Regent of the Universe. Those baby shoulders became burdened shoulders. Those cross scarred shoulders are broad shoulders. He came back from the dead to be the Governor.

A. In Matthew 28:19-20 we read the realms of His government. "All authority..."

1. In Heaven
Philippians 2 declares that "God hath highly exalted Him." Ephesians 1 declares that He reigns above all in the heavens.
2. Here on Earth
Jesus Christ has power on this earth.
3. In Hell
All satanic power has been defeated by our Governor.
4. In the Heart
He has the right to rule in your heart.

B. Why should Jesus be Governor of your life?

1. He took your burden on His broad shoulders. No one else could bear your sin burden.
2. He loves you.
3. Your present governor will take you to hell!
4. Jesus has the right to do it. He shed His blood to buy you back from the oppressor.

C. What is life like under our Governor?

1. His kingdom will never end.
2. His constitution is the Bible.
3. His enemies are defeated.
4. His subjects live forever in heaven.
5. His courts are glorious.

Conclusion:

The shoulders that bore the cross bear also the ensign of Ruler. In Isaiah 22:15-25, we read how God stripped away the authority of Shebna and gave it to Eliakim. In that passage (22:22), God says, "The key of the house of David I will lay on His shoulder; so he shall open and no one shall shut, and he shall shut, and no one shall open." Revelation 3:7 cites this verse and declares that truth fulfilled in Jesus. Jesus has and holds the keys.

> He holds the keys,
> He holds the keys;
> Though we've been held captive,
> At long last we are free,
> For He holds the keys.

Who can forget the words of Luke 15:5 that states that when the searching shepherd finds the straying sheep, "He lays it on His shoulders rejoicing." Yes, the cross was laid on His shoulders. The keys of authority are on His shoulders. Praise God, there is room for a lost sinner on His shoulders.

In the swimming pool, there is a game played by young people. Two big people put smaller people on their shoulders. Then the two teams battle each other. The object is for one rider to dislodge the other into the water. I always had to be "the shoulders." Many times I lost my young warrior. But listen, Jesus has never lost one! Once you are on His shoulders you are on your way Home.

— ✧ —

Sermon 8

THE KING'S WONDERFUL NAME
Isaiah 9:6-7

Introduction:

Seven hundred forty years before Jesus was born, the statesman-prophet, Isaiah, encouraged his war-torn nation with this inspired prophecy. "These dark clouds are to be replaced with a royal light. The disgrace will be turned into glory. The burden is to be lifted. The battle is to end and the weapons of war are to be burned."

Who is it that heralds through this age of glory? Isaiah looks through the telescope of prophecy and sees the new age dawning in the coming of a new King. A child is to be born. This pictures Jesus, the "ancient of days" who became *infant of days*. The *creator Christ* became the *cradled Christ*. God became flesh in the virgin womb of Mary and was born into the world.

Also "a Son is given." This pictures the cross of Christ. He was a love gift to the world. Heaven kissed earth in the coming of Jesus. Royal blood flowed through the veins of Jesus—blood which would be shed for our sins.

A soldier was on the operating table in the hospital tent during World War II. The surgeon said to him, "Son, we have to take your leg." "No, sir," said the boy, "You are not taking it; I am giving it for my country." That's what Jesus said, "No man takes my life, I lay it down willingly."

Not only do we see His Cradle and His Cross, but also His Crown. "The government shall be upon His shoulders." He is Lord. After death, Jesus comes forth as Lord. That's our Jesus. Before the government could be upon His shoulders, there had to be a rugged cross upon His shoulders. The shoulders that bore the cross now have the authority over all of creation upon them.

The government of individual people's lives can be upon His shoulders. When you give your life to Christ, He takes

45

the government of your life upon His shoulders. He comes into your life as "Wonderful, Counselor, the Mighty God, the Everlasting Father, the Prince of Peace." Some say that these titles are four names. The Hebrew scholar, Delitzch, says that they are really five names. In these names, we see the wonderful privilege of having Jesus in our hearts:

I. **His Name Is Wonderful:**
    He Gives Contentment in Life.

The word "wonderful" means *unique, separate, miraculous,* and *amazing*. It is Jesus who gives life the glow of wonder. How sad it is when life is monotonous, dull and unfulfilling. Jesus gives lasting contentment. His wonderful life, words, death and resurrection make our life wonderful.

I feel sorry for people whose lives hold no surprises. There is mystery even in knowing Jesus. He fills our lives with wonder. Each day gives birth to new life when you know Christ. Life with all of its problems is an adventure when you follow Christ by faith.

Isn't that the wonder of Christmas? God surprised the world when He sent Jesus the way He did. He surprised Mary and Joseph. The shepherds had the surprise of their lives when they heard the angelic voices herald His coming. The Eastern kings were surprised by a strange phenomenon in the heavens. It is still a wonder—that which Jesus does in the hearts of those who trust Him.

I think that many have replaced making a life with making a living. Buying a house has replaced building a home. When are we going to learn that we cannot enjoy the things money can buy,if we lose the things money can't buy.

II. **His Name Is Counselor:**
     He Gives Us Counsel for Life.

Our lives are filled with choices. Every day we face decisions. How can we know what to do? We must look to our counselor! "Thou shalt guide me with thy counsel, and afterward receive me to glory" (Ps.73:24). When are we going to learn this? People will write Dear Abby, read books, go to unsaved psychiatrists and talk to everybody they know except the One who can help them! I know Jesus will help you, because He loves you, because He is praying for you, because He has given us a book filled with His wisdom. When this book says no, it is God saying don't hurt yourself. When it gives a promise, it is God saying, "Help yourself to blessings."

III. His Name Is Mighty God: He Gives Us Courage for Living.

This name means invincible and victorious. The word mighty is used elsewhere of the conquering hero. This is what Jesus is to us. He has conquered life, facing its tests and temptations; so can we. He has conquered sin, having put it to death on the cross, and broken its power by forgiving us. He has conquered death, leaving its scepter and crown shattered in an empty tomb, and now has broken down its gates, and holds its keys in His hand.

This Jesus lives in me. He gives me courage and hope in the midst of all of life's enemies.

IV. His Name Is Everlasting Father: He Gives Us Care.

He is described as "Father for eternity." This describes Jesus as one of loving provision and concern for His children. He who rules the vastness of eternity, He whose life stretches from everlasting to everlasting also cares for me as a Father.

> Oh yes, He cares, I know He cares.
> His heart is touched with my grief.
> When the days are weary,
> The long nights dreary,
> I know my Savior cares.

V. His Name Is Prince of Peace: He Gives Us Calmness.

The Hebrew here is *Sar-Shalom*. Jesus is the embodiment of peace. Jesus gives us peace in our hearts now and one day, at His coming, He will give a new world that be peaceful. Peace is the cessation of hostilities in the heart of the believer. It is the surrender of life to Jesus. It is living life on His terms.

Some think peace is quiet. Some think peace is like a graveyard. Some think the face of a sleeping newborn infant pictures peace. Not so. Peace is not quiet, nor death, nor innocence. Peace is that sense of calmness and well-being that fills our lives regardless of how loud, difficult, or confusing life may be. It is the signed treaty of surrender to our Lord Jesus. When the Prince of Peace reigns in your heart, the peace of God rules in your life!

Conclusion:

Does this Jesus live in your heart? The Christ of the *cradle*, the Christ of the *cross,* is the Christ of *Christmas.* He is the crowned Christ. Has He received a personal crowning in your life? Is the government of your life upon His shoulder? Has He come into your life as your all in all? Everything that He did, He did for you. Everything He has, He desires to give you. He will give you contentment, calmness, courage and counsel for living.

Aren't you tired of cheap substitutes—amusements cannot replace joy. Worldly propaganda cannot replace truth. Manufactured and packaged experiences cannot rescue you from a boring, dull and guilty existence. Only Jesus can give your life meaning. His Name is Wonderful!

> Unto us a child is given,
> Something strange and stranger,
> The King of Kings and Lord of Lords,
> An Infant in a manger,
> His name shall be called wonderful.
> The Child is meek and lowly,
> The Comforter, the Prince of Peace,
> Holy, Holy, Holy.
>   - Marie King

I KNOW A NAME

I know a soul that is steeped in sin,
    That no man's art can cure;
But I know a Name, a Name, a Name
    That can make that soul all pure.

I know a life that is lost to God,
    Bound down by the things of earth;
But I know a Name, a Name, a Name
    That can bring that soul new birth.

I know of lands that are sunk in shame,
    Of hearts that faint and tire;
But I know a Name, a Name, a Name
    That can set those lands on fire.

Its sound is a brand, its letters flame,
    Like glowing tongues of fire.
I know a Name, a Name, a Name
    Of which the world ne'er tires.

- Anonymous

— ✧ —

Sermon 9

DAY OF RECKONING
Isaiah 9:8-10:34

Introduction:

This section of Isaiah was written during that first great crisis in Isaiah's ministry, the Syro-Ephraimitic Crisis. Remember, Assyria was the world power in 73 B.C. Their armies under Tiglath-Pileser were marching toward the southwest through Syria and Israel toward Egypt. Rezin, king of Syria and Pekah, pseudo-king of Israel (the Northern Kingdom) had formed an alliance to battle Tiglath. Ahaz, king of Judah, reached out to Assyria rather than trusting God. Judah would face severe trials because of this faith failure.

Israel would fare far worse, going into Assyrian captivity. Only a small remnant would return. These verses clearly demonstrate God's awesome judgment on nations that refuse to acknowledge Him.

That day of intrigue, treaties, war and peace is contemporary. Petty tyrants like Tiglath and Pekah are present today. Pekah was not of the royal line of Israel. He had murdered the rightful king in a military coup and taken power. Israel had allowed this tyrant to reign as king. Our day has seen its share of tyrants and dictators. A world that rejects the claims of Jehovah and disdains His leadership will suffer under Satan emissaries. When will we learn that God almighty is sovereign in this world. Three serious matters should claim our undivided attention in these Scriptures:

I. God's Verdict on the Nation's Faith (9:8-10:4)

Isaiah 10:3-19 describes "a day of reckoning" (NIV). What brings on disaster to a people? Throughout these verses we find a refrain that is repeated (9:12,17,21; 10:4). The refrain says, "Yet for all of this His anger is not turned away; His hand is still upraised."

God is astonished that the nation will not return. What is it that causes a nation to fall under the discipline of the Almighty? They are the same things that keep individuals from coming to Christ!

1.   Unresponsive Will (9:8-12)
Israel refused the loving call of Jehovah's discipline. Why? Verse 9 relates the cause—arrogance and pride. When God said, "I will," they said, "We will."

The reason many of you will not respond to Christ is because you simply do not want to.   The reason many believers are having difficulty with relationships is pride. Wounded pride, if nursed, will drive you away from the Lord and people.

2.   Unrepentant Heart (9:13-17)
Look at 9:13 and see the second problem that brought on the day of reckoning. The nation's problems had not caused them to return to God. There was no hunger for God. They had no desire to seek the Lord.

How sad it is when our reversals do not bring us to repentance. How important it is that our difficulties bring us to devotion! Do your problems bring you to God or drive you away? Are you seeking the Lord?

3.   Unrighteous Life (9:18-21)
Verse 18 indicates the third reality of God's reckoning—wickedness. Alexander Pope, in tracing the deterioration of a life, says, "We first endure, then pity, then embrace." This was true of Israel. It is true of all people. When God's message gets no response, then soon the unrepentant person goes deeper into sin.

4.   Unreliable Actions (10:1-4)
The final indication that judgment is near is a heartlessness toward the less fortunate.   Society becomes cruel to the most vulnerable and helpless.   Woe unto the nation or individual who has lost integrity and compassion.

II. God's View of the Nation's Foe (10:5-19)

In this section, God has a dialogue through the prophet with the mighty kingdom of Assyria. This nation, that caused kingdoms to tremble, is viewed differently by God.

Assyria is simply a "rod" in God's hand (vs. 5). God

sent Assyria to war (6-7). Assyria was an "axe" in God's hand (vs. 15). First, we need to recognize the sovereignty of God in the world. No nation moves without God's permission. Second, war and invasion are judgments of God. Third, God's will shall be done!

Assyria was in the firm grip of the Almighty and did not know it (10:5, 15). Their day of reckoning would come soon. Isaiah 37:33-38 records the awful end of the Assyrian dynasty. Isaiah prophesied in Isaiah 10:17 that in a single day God would deliver Jerusalem from the Assyrians. Read the story in Isaiah 37:33-38. One angel took care of the pride of Assyria.

Do you feel your enemies are too strong for God? Are your problems too immense for Him? Only pride will keep you from falling before Him.

III. God's Vision for the Nation's Future (10:20-34)

The key phrase in these verses is "that day."
1.   Day of Reliance (20)
Isaiah looked forward to a day when people would live by faith in God, relying on His word.
2.   Day of Return (21-22)
The promise of the remnant is God's word to Israel that, as a people, they will survive. Indeed they have returned to God from three captivities!

Dear friend, if God can restore Israel, He can restore your life. David cried out in Psalm 23, "He restoreth my soul."
3.   Day of Relief (10:27)
God takes away the burden and yoke of sin. Here, our Lord fulfills this promise as He cries, "Come unto me all ye that labor and are heavy laden and I will give thee rest. Take my yoke upon you and learn of me for I am meek and lowly of heart and ye shall find rest unto your souls" (Matthew 11:28).
4.   Day of Rescue (10:28-34)
These closing verses picture the invading army driving toward Jerusalem. When they arrive they are astonished, for they look upon Mt. Zion and see God's people. Then

they hear God's people say, "See the Lord, the Lord almighty," and the enemy is defeated.

Oh, beloved, what a picture of salvation—the believer safe with the Lord! What an elevation—the believer on the mountain with the Lord. What inspiration—as all foes fall before the sword of His word.

Conclusion:

Are you willing to come to Him? Are you willing to see your pride broken? Isn't it time for you to return to the Lord?

— ✧ —

THE ROOTS OF HISTORY'S HOPE
Isaiah 11:1-16

Introduction:

The story of Eugene Lang gives us an ultimate example of the power of hope. Entrepreneur Lang was featured as *Successful Man of the Year* by *SUCCESS* magazine in 1986. The following is a part of a feature article about Lang's encouragement of others.

A distinguished gray haired man stands alone in the center of the auditorium stage, his paternal presence sporting a fine wool suit and the barest trace of a mustache. He scans the sunlit room, with its peeling paint and frayed draperies, but his gaze lingers on the people.

They are black and Hispanic men and women who fill most of the seats in the auditorium. Though some do not speak English, their attention is fixed on the man at the podium. However, his speech is not aimed at them. He has returned to this place, where he once was a student, to address the sixty-one sixth graders, dressed in blue caps and gowns, who are seated in the front rows. "This is your first graduation—just the perfect time to dream," he says. "Dream of what you want to be, the kind of life you wish to build, and believe in that dream. Be prepared to work for it. Always remember, each dream is important because it is your dream, it is your future. And it is worth working for."

"You must study," he continues. "You must learn. You must attend junior high school, high school, and then college. You can go to college. You must go to college. Stay in school and I'll..." The speaker pauses and then, as if suddenly inspired, he blurts out: "I will give each of you a college scholarship."

For a second there is silence, and then a wave of emotion rolls over the crowd. The people in the auditorium are on their feet, jumping and running, cheering and waving and hugging one another. Parents rush down the aisles to their children. "What did he say?" one mother calls out in Spanish. "It's money! Money for college!" her daughter yells back with delight, collapsing into her parent's arms.

The place was an elementary school in a poverty stricken, drug-ridden, despair-plagued Harlem neighborhood. The speaker was multimillionaire entrepreneur Eugene Lang, who fifty-three years earlier had graduated from that very school. The date was June 25, 1981, and the big question was whether the warm and ever-confident Lang, a man who believes that "each individual soul is of infinite worth and infinite dignity," would fulfill his promise.

Well, he did and he still is fulfilling it. In fact, these kids are now getting ready to graduate from high school and only one of them has dropped out of high school since the sixth grade. You have to understand, in this community, ninety percent of the kids drop out of high school.

That wonderful story speaks of the power of hope! It is hope that is the hallmark of Christianity. The ancient mythological religions and most world religions look backward and not forward. In Biblical Christianity, we are forever looking forward to things to come.

Isaiah 10 ended with Israel cut down by Assyria. Staring at the stump of a ruined Israel would seem to mean despair. Yet there is life in stump and roots. Isaiah 11:1 says, "There shall come forth..." Look at Isaiah 11:11. "It shall come to pass..."

God writes the last chapter of history. God always saves the best for last! The hope of Israel is the hope of the world, the Messiah. Isaiah 11 speaks of the coming of Jesus. He is a branch (1:1) and a banner (11:11-12). He is David's son (11:1) and David's sovereign (11:10). He is Lord of war (11:15-16) and Prince of Peace (11:6-9). He is the coming King. He has now come and yet He is to come again. This passage speaks of the vast panorama of the two advents of Christ into the world. He alone is the herald of hope to the world and to the heart! The hope that we have in Jesus is deeply rooted in four areas:

I. **Rooted in Scriptural Prophecy** (11:1, 11)

The great prophetic theme of the Bible is the coming of Jesus. When you venture out of Isaiah, you can journey all the way back east of Eden and hear the promise to our ancient parents, the coming of "the seed of woman." Every blood sacrifice of the Old Testament pointed its crimson tide toward Calvary. Every echo of the thundering judgments of Sinai cried out for Calvary.

Old Testament prophecy says He is coming. New Testament Scripture says He has come and He shall come again. Beyond that, He can come now into your heart.

You see, God's kingdom is already here as an invisible force (See Luke 17:20-21). Whenever Jesus is acknowledged as Lord, the kingdom has come. Matt. 6:33 says, "Seek first the kingdom of God and His righteousness, and all these things shall be added to you." This is not a call to seek heaven later, but a call to live under the kingship of Jesus now. It is our quest to live now in His invisible kingdom until the literal kingdom comes.

II. **Rooted in Israel's Destiny** (11:1-2, 11-16)

The roots of our Redeemer are a part of the tree of Israel. God's chosen people have been the bearers of God's message to us. In the last days, and especially after the rapture of the church, the elect of Israel will return to the Messiah. Today many Jews have returned to the land, but at the end they will return to the Lord.

In 11:11-16, the promise of a national return to the land of Israel is clearly predicted. Such a deliverance will be likened unto the delivery of the nation from Egypt.

Israel is God's timepiece on the nations. As the old Roman Empire reassembles in a unified Europe, the focus of history will shift dramatically to the Middle East. Inevitably, Israel will turn to the Messiah, Jesus, and evangelize the tribulation torn world.

III. **Rooted in Human Tragedy** (11:3-9)

The world needs King Jesus. His reign will end the trail of tears we call human history. Isaiah 11:3-5 promises an end to the abuse of the poor and equity for the meek. He promises an end to the terrors of the wicked.

When Jesus reigns during the Millennium, every human tragedy will vanish. The curse will be lifted and the animals will lose their savage instincts. Children will be safe from man and beast.

In those ancient kingdoms, unwanted children were simply discarded. Even in the Roman Empire they would simply be abandoned on the side of a road and often eaten by wild dogs.

God promises safety for the children from the savage spirit of man and beast. The earth will be full of people who know the Lord (Isaiah 11:9). The heartache of human tragedy will be at an end.

IV. **Rooted in Divine Mercy** (11:10, 16)

Human hope is rooted in the mercy of God. He is our banner of hope (11:10). A banner was either a flag or an image on a pole around which people gathered. Jesus is our banner of hope.

In John 3:14, we are told of Moses lifting up the brazen banner of the serpent. Every dying Jew who had been the victim of the serpent's bite could look and live. John said, "As Moses lifted up the serpent in the wilderness, even so must the son of man be lifted up" (John 3:14). Jesus was lifted up for our sins, and now we march under the banner of the cross.

Who can forget the thrilling story of our national anthem. As a prisoner on a ship, Frances Scott Key watched through the long night. Finally, he saw the flag still waving, and hope for freedom filled his heart as he penned the national anthem.

Listen, our banner still stands. We have a "resting place" (Isaiah 11:10). A glorious gathering place is ours around our dear crucified and risen Savior.

> The cross, it standeth fast,
> Hallelujah, Hallelujah!
> Defying every blast,
> Hallelujah, Hallelujah!

> The winds of hell have blown,
>   The world its hate has shown,
> But the cross is not o'er thrown,
>   Hallelujah for the cross!

Conclusion:

God's kingdom is invisible now, but inevitable in power. His kingdom is available to you today. You must decide who will be your king, either Christ or Satan. The kingdom of Christ is invincible! His kingdom will come on earth as it is in heaven.

— ✧ —

Sermon 11

THE WELLS OF SALVATION
Isaiah 12:1-6

Introduction:

In America, we are blessed with an abundance of clear water. We can go to the tap and receive water at any time. Water is a precious commodity that we take for granted. This was not so in Israel. Water was a priceless treasure. Life flourished where there was an abundance of water.

I can remember an occasion when I realized the value of water. In 1978, I spent twenty days in the Philippines. My ministry was centered in the rural region of the island of Mindanao. There was no running water. Each day a journey was made to the community well where buckets were lowered and raised by hand. Families had certain times to bathe at the well. I was not allowed to go to the well. I hired two young people to bring me two buckets of water. One I would bathe with and the other I would boil to drink. This ritual took two full hours everyday I was in the bush. I remember how angry I got the day a pig knocked over my water bucket and ate the only bar of soap within twenty-five miles!

Where there is no water there is no life! Water became a symbol of life and salvation in Israel. Isaiah 12:1-6 records one of Israel's favorite songs built on the theme of the wells of salvation.

I. **Salvation Explained** (1-2)

Note that salvation is desperately needed by humanity. Verse 1 speaks of the anger of God. Psalm 7:11 says, "God is angry with the wicked every day." The word "wrath" in the Bible translates a word which means *intense, abiding anger*. Among the attributes of a Holy God is an anger against sin. Notice Isaiah says, "You were angry with me" (vs. 1). God is angry with the sin, not with the person. Anger does not eliminate love.

What was it that turned away the Lord's anger? It was faith in God's forgiving power. To the Old Testament Jew, it was God's mighty acts of deliverance celebrated and illustrated in the rituals. The sacrifices answered the demand of an angry and outraged heaven. Faith is the power of God to save and the willingness of God to save.

Isaiah 12:2 is a hymn chorus repeatedly used in the history of Israel. In Exodus 15:2, these exact words express the Joy of Israel upon the occasion of their deliverance through the Red Sea. Yahweh had kept His promise to save the people. Now they stood in victory with their enemies drowned in the sea.

The same stanza is found in Psalm 118:14. This Psalm is a post-exilic Psalm written upon the occasion of Israel's return from Babylonian captivity. Again, it is the Lord who has saved.

Dr. Leo Green is right when he sets forth three wonderful truths about Yahweh in this verse: He is our salvation, our strength, and our song! The Lord is the well of our salvation.

Today we do not see God's mightiest act in terms of the return from Egypt through the Red Sea, nor the return from Babylonian captivity. We live on this side of Calvary, God's mightiest act where the wrath of the Father fell upon the Son. The anger of God against sinners has been met by the blood of Jesus Christ. Salvation takes place when you say as Isaiah, "I will trust and not be afraid."

II. **Salvation Experienced** (12:3)

Verse 3 moves from the explanation of salvation to the experience of salvation. How does one experience salvation? Please note these three things:

1. Provision - The image of a well is used in this verse. Imagine yourself going days without water in dry desert land. You are thirsty, dirty, and dying. You crest a hill and see a grove of palm trees. You rush down to discover a well of fresh, cool water. Soon you are pouring buckets of water over your body. Cool water flows down your parched throat and life is restored. Without Christ, we are thirsty, dirty and dying! God has "wells" of salvation.

There is an abundant provision for all who will come.
2. Process - Not only is there provision, there is a process. We must draw the water. God has provided the bucket of faith. Only a fool would stare at the well, study the well, or stand around the well dying of thirst. We must drop the bucket of faith. You will never exhaust Jesus.
3. Praise - There will also be praise, for drawing from the well of salvation brings joy. Do you remember the woman at Jacob's well in John 4? She came to Jesus, spiritually thirsty, sinfully dirty, and tragically alienated. The women in those days journeyed to the well together, usually singing joyfully. Jesus, sitting on the well curb without a bucket, said, "give me a drink." She was shocked that this Jew spoke to her. Then Jesus said, "If you know the gift of God and who it is who says to you give me a drink, you would have asked Him and He would have given you living water" (John 4:10). She reminded Jesus, "You have nothing to draw with." She was right, He was the well. She had the bucket of faith. She wanted to argue race and religion. Jesus said to her, "If you take the water I give you, you will never thirst again" (John 4:14a). She believed and was saved.

In John 7:37-38, Jesus is watching the ceremony of the feast of the tabernacles. The Jews are celebrating water from the Rock that sustained their forefathers in the wilderness. They had journeyed to the brook Kidron, filled their golden vessels and poured them out before the people singing Isaiah 12:3, "with joy shall we draw water out of the wells of salvation." At that very moment Jesus shouted, "If any man thirst let him come to me and drink and out of his inner most being shall flow rivers of living water." John goes on to say that Jesus was speaking of the work of the Holy Spirit in the heart of the believer.

III. **Salvation Expressed** (12:4-6)

Salvation must be shared if it is genuine. The joy of knowing Christ should overflow from the Christian life.
1. Salvation is expressed best by a people of praise and prayer.

2. Salvation is shared best by a people who know His power and preeminence.

3. Salvation is expressed by a people who unashamedly acknowledge His presence.

We must "declare His deeds among the people" (vs. 4). Our abiding joy and song is, the Lord saves! How can we remain sad and silent in view of God's great salvation?

Conclusion: Salvation Expected

This great chorus was sung by Moses at the Red Sea. It was sung by an exiled people returning home from captivity. It was sung by a priesthood as empty as the vessels they held in their hands. It was sung by a prophet longing for Emmanuel. It has been sung by untold numbers across the centuries. Yet, we shall sing it again. Revelation 15:1-4 records that scene—God's redeemed, standing by a sea of glass with harps of gold, singing the song of victory.

> When this poor lisping stammering tongue
> Lies silent in the grave,
> Then in a nobler, sweeter song
> I'll sing Thy power to save.

> \- William Cowper

— ✧ —

Sermon 12

WHEN THE STARS REFUSE TO SHINE
Isaiah 13:1-22

Introduction:

A highly educated religious leader lectured to a local religious body recently. He predicted that the millennium could possibly be at hand. He sees the present movements toward reunification in Europe, the changes in Soviet Russia, and other events as bringing in the millennium. He says that this would come in fulfillment of Jewish hopes.

Let me say that I believe the millennium is coming, but it will not be ushered in on the shoulders of this world system. The millennium will come when the Messiah, the Lord Jesus Christ, returns. Before Jesus returns to reign, He will raise the dead and translate the living believer to glory. Then one awful judgment will come upon the world.

Isaiah has just prophesied the coming of Emmanuel. Immediately, he moves from the blessing of the world to the burden of the world. Isaiah 13-23 lists ten nations that faced the judgment of God for various sins.

This section, though historical and practical, stretches from eternity to eternity. There is in these temporal judgments a typical and prophetical view of the wrath to come. The sins of the nations are seen as the result of fallen human nature. Yet, the mystery of Lucifer and his fall is found in this section. We shall look at the eternal principles that apply to us today.

The first burden is of Babylon. That name is prominent in Biblical history and prophecy. Babylon is a byword for *rebellion against God*. A rebellion begins in Genesis 11 and ends in Revelation 18.

In Isaiah's day, it was a rising world power that would eventually overthrow the Assyrian Empire. Nebuchadnezzar was its best known king. Later, as prophesied in this text, Babylon would fall to the Medes and the Persians.

In this section, there are three clear truths we need to understand. We must:

I. Understand God and His Word (13:1-2)

When God gets ready to say something to this world, He raises up a preacher. Isaiah "saw" what God was about to do. He was a man of vision who knew God and could see what God was up to on this planet.

Real preaching comes from a man of vision. Isaiah knew God and he knew the world in which he lived. He could see clearly what God was about to do. He also had a grasp of eternal and ultimate reality. He could see beyond the moments of his age to the future.

The message Isaiah shared is called a *burden*. The Hebrew word *nasa* comes from a word which means *to carry a heavy load*. It means the message of God is weighty and heavy. Isaiah was willing to be God's heavy-weight! He came with the truth even though it was heavy.

It is difficult to be a prophet in times of prosperity. It is much easier to speak the blessing and not the burden. How easy it is to tell this generation that they are bringing in the millennium, However, in this world, I do not see the light of hope, but the darkness of paganism.

II. Understand God and His World (3-5)

If Isaiah teaches us anything it is that God is sovereign over the nations. Satan may be the god of this age, but "the earth is the Lord's and the fullness thereof." Situations that are beyond humanity's control are never beyond God's control. In this section, God calls the nations by name, and he calls their sins by name.

Thus, nations not only live under the sovereignty of God, but they also live in accountability to God. What is true of nations is true of individuals. Sin will be judged.

In surveying these eleven chapters, we discover six prominent sins that destroy nations. These sins are rooted in rejection of God and His word:

1. The sin of debauchery - Babylon
This includes sex, alcohol, drugs, and related sins.

2. The sin of anti-semitism - Philistia, Arabia
3. The sin of pride - Moab (16:6)
4. The sin of inhumanity - Syria, Ethiopia, Edom
5. The sin of occultism - Egypt (19:2-4, 11)
6. The sin of materialism - Tyre

[These are the sins that will characterize the last days.]

III. **Understand God and His Wrath** (13:6-22)

There are several very practical truths about the wrath of God. First, God's wrath is both present and coming. Verses 6-16 speak of the future wrath while verses 17-22 speak of the more immediate judgment on Babylon at the hand of the Medes. God's eternal hatred of sin and the curse upon this earth allow us to live in a damned world where we are subject to war, disease, terror and death.

Secondly, God's wrath is fearful. In that day, destruction will come. Fear, pain, travail and fever describe those who face God's wrath. Even the galaxies and stars will be affected by the stirring of an angry God rising in judgment! This description warns all humanity of the awful fate of those who reject God.

Third, God's wrath is final. Verses 17-22 describe some ancient cities that were judged. Sodom and Gomorrah have never been located. God wiped them off the earth.

Conclusion:

In the last days, a resurrected Babylon will meet its ultimate doom as God judges the world for its rejection of His Son, Christ. In this burdened message is there any hope? Look at 13:1-3. God has sent the preacher to warn and to call them to repentance. God is gathering His people together before the day of wrath. Who are those who are safe from wrath? "Those who rejoice in my exaltation" (13:3). Look at Isaiah 25:1-5. He can be your God, your strength, your shade, and your refuge. You can trust Emmanuel, the Lord Jesus Christ.

— ✧ —

Sermon 13

Two Perilous Principles
Isaiah 14:3-15

Introduction:

Isaiah 14:3-14 reveals two startling principles of evil that have operated through the ages in all nations. One is the Babylonian principle that dates from the tower of Babel. In fact, the word Babylon found in Isaiah is Babel according to Franz Delitsch. The other principle is the Luciferian principle. Lucifer is the pre-fall name of Satan.

In every generation, there are nations that reflect like a mirror these two principles. These two principles and those who live by them are marching inexorably toward judgment.

I. The Babylonian Principle (14:3-10)

This is the principle of human government that attempts to rule without God. When you turn to Genesis 10:9-10, you read the origins of human government and of this Babylonian principle. Notice the descent of Noah through Cush was Nimrod. Nimrod was the first king of Babel. He was on the throne when the building of the tower was initiated. It was under Nimrod that we first see human fame applauded. Nimrod was the first to try to unify fallen humanity. It was Nimrod who became the god of a new religion. Revelation 17:5 calls it "Mystery Babylon, the mother of harlots." The church is the bride and every other religion is a harlot. A harlot is an imitation, a hired bride!

Nimrod's wife was named Semirimis and they had a son named Baal. Baal was killed by a wild boar, and they claimed he was raised from the dead forty days thereafter. Later, it was believed that he was hatched out of an egg.

From this beginning, a mother-child cult spread across the world. There were Diane and Cupid, and Atenis and

Eros. Every nation became infected with this cult. Other nations called this mother-child cult Ishtar and Baal.

The remnants of that cult remain even in the language we Christians use. The word *Easter* comes from Ishtar or Ashtaroth. Forty days of lent are not in the Bible—that is Baalism.

The worship of mother Mary or mother earth is no more than a carryover from this cult.

The principle of Babel relies upon man's works, religion, science, and ingenuity. This principle desires to dethrone God and deify humanity. Throughout history, human rulers eventually claim deity—the *pharaohs, the caesars, Hitler* and *Lenin.* The world will eventually fall before the offspring of this evil principle, Antichrist.

Paul called this evil principle "the mystery of iniquity" (See II Thessalonians 2:1-12). At the end of the age, false religion will ride the "beast" of human government (Revelation 17:3). Efforts at world unity, regardless of how well intentioned, will end up hating God and His Gospel.

Babylonian government is oppressive (vs.4), materialistic (vs. 4), cruel (vs. 6), and doomed (vs. 9-11).

II. The Luciferian Principle (12-21)

This passage is a prophecy of the fall of the king of Babylon. Yet, again it reflects the king of hell, Satan. The early church fathers were the first to tie this passage to our Lord's statement in Luke, "I saw Satan fall like lightening from heaven." Here Satan is called Lucifer or Daystar. It means *herald of the dawn* or *lightbearer.*

Lucifer was one of the prominent angels mentioned in Scripture with Gabriel and Michael. Gabriel is God's herald angel. He anchors the news of heaven. Michael is God's warrior angel. He is captain of the hosts. Lucifer was God's angel placed over all of creation. He was both seraphim which means *burning one* or *brilliant one*, and cherubim which has to do with the *government at creation.*

Ezekiel 28:11-27 describes his function. He has to seal and cover the creation of God. He was to lead in praise to God. He was beautifully colored and made beautiful melody. It was Lucifer who played the melody and put on

a fireworks display on creation morning "when the morning
stars sang together and the sons of God shouted for joy"
(See Job). Somewhere between Genesis 1:1 and Genesis 1:2
a terrible catastrophe befell heaven and earth. Satan fell
and ruined creation. "And the earth was without form, and
void; and darkness was upon the face of the deep" (Genesis
1:2).

We can only catch a glimpse of what happened in that
awful moment . He was the angel of worship (Ezekiel 28).
He walked in the glory. What happened? Here is the
Lucifer principle. It is pride. Isaiah 1 records the five "*I
will's*" of Satan. Look at this principle that operated in
Adam and plunged the whole race toward hell.

1. "I will ascend to heaven." - Satan desired God's
power for the wrong motive.

2. "I will exalt my throne." - He desired God's *place*.

3. "I will sit on the mount of the congregation." -
Satan wanted God's *people*.

4. "I will ascend above the heights of the clouds." -
Satan desired the *preeminence* of God. He wanted the glory
reserved for God above.

5. "I will be like the most high." - Satan wanted the
program of God without His person.

You see, man in his pride buys into this principle. Man
wants power, place, people, preeminence, and program
without bowing to the God of heaven. We want everything
but the person of God.

Pride is a peculiar thing. It despises God and whomev-
er God may choose to use. A.W. Tozer was right when he
said, "Whole, unbroken men are of little use to God."

I read about a study at Auburn University on milk
cows. It seems *old bossy* is a good name for the milk cow.
It was found that cows in large milking centers were giving
less milk. After an intensive study, it was discovered that
these cows have to establish a milking order. So they moo
and bellow and twitch their tails at each other, competing
for position. Monitors placed on the cows showed that they
were stressed out due to this constant wrangling. These
cows, it was discovered, could smell each other and that is
what started it. So they started squirting a licorice mixture

on the cows so they could not smell each other. The result was less stress and more milk.

You say, how silly. Yes, but how human-like. In our pride, we jockey for position and place. In our pride, we get upset with others who do not *smell* or *look* like we do. We become less productive. Pride is a deadly and damning sin.

Conclusion:

These two principles we call *humanism* and *pride*. They are the two-headed enemy of your soul. Humble yourself before God. Admit your need for Jesus Christ. Turn from this world system to Christ.

— ◇ —

Sermon 14

THE BURDEN OF THE WORLD
Context: Isaiah 15:1-19:25
Text: Isaiah 17:10-18:4

Introduction:

Years ago, there was a heavyweight championship boxing match between Mike Tyson, the champ at that time, and an unknown boxer named Douglas. All of the prognosticators predicted a Tyson victory. Surprisingly, Douglas got up off the floor and knocked Tyson out to become the champion. The unlikely happened!

Today, it may seem that the cause of God is taking a beating. Never fear; when the smoke clears away, Jesus Christ will be wearing the diadem of the ages.

The *burden* section of Isaiah speaks of the heaviness of judgment that sin brings on the nations. Certainly, the nations mentioned have experienced temporal judgments. Yet, this section reaches far beyond Isaiah's day, and ultimately to what the Scripture calls "that day."

Here, we find Moab (Jordan), Damascus (Syria), Cush (Ethiopia), Egypt, Assyria, and Israel mentioned. Assyria, under Tiglath-Pileser, and Sargon II conquered all of these nations between 740 and 700 B.C. These immediate judgments took place as God promised. In the midst of these warnings, there are prophetical warnings and truths we dare not miss. They are described in the following outline affirmed by God's word:

1. The world rejects God.
2. The Jews return to Israel.
3. The church raptured to glory.
4. The world ruined by the tribulation.
5. The king returns to reign a thousand years.
6. Peace comes to the world at last.
   [All of these truths are found in these scriptures.]

73

I. The Burden Revealed

A cursory survey of these five chapters clearly reveals the burden the world lives under. Let me make it very clear that the cause of this burden is sin! God has structured the universe that way. Paul tells us in Romans 6, "The wages of sin is death." He also states that "Whosoever commits sin is the servant of sin." Proverbs 13:15 says, "The way of a transgressor is hard." Please note the consequences of sin revealed in these Scriptures:

1. Nations without peace (15:1-8)
2. Problems without answers (16:3, 19:3)
3. Religion without power (16:9-13) Religion will do anything but hear and honor the Word of God.
4. Church without the glory (17:4)
5. World without God (17:10)

These consequences are an exact prophecy of the signs of the end of the age. Now listen carefully to me. This burden is our message. We are to warn this present age of the danger it faces in the future.

The consummation of this burden is inevitable. In Isaiah 16:13, we discover that nothing can avail to save the reprobated nations. Their doom is inevitable. Listen to me friends. This world as we know it, is doomed. Nothing will save this world system. However, though the world faces a terrible burden, individuals can have their burden removed. You may be living with problems you can't solve, war instead of peace, religion without power, church without glory, in a world without God, but there is hope. Look again and see:

II. The Burden Removed

Hidden away in these chapters are wonderful promises that will lift your burden. First, Jesus must be enthroned as Lord (16:5). One day He will reign during the millennium and the world's dark night will be over. In the meantime you must enthrone Him now in your heart. Notice, love is the reason for Jesus coming. He will reign in faithfulness, and will never fail nor disappoint you.

Second, understand that God has already said all He

needs to say concerning the future. In Isaiah 18:3-4, we find that God's next sound will be a trumpet sounding the rapture and calling forth the judgment. God says, "He will remain quiet" (Isaiah 18:4 NIV).

Third, realize *this day* can never be *that day*. *This day* sees the middle east in turmoil—*that day* will see the Arab world and Israel bowing before God (Isaiah 19:23-25).

Conclusion:

Though lasting peace cannot come until Christ comes, you can have peace in your heart. God will remove your burden of sin. When God became a man, He took your burden on His back in the form of a cross. At Calvary even drops of Jesus' blood broke the oppressive power of sin and Satan. Isaiah 17:7 speaks of a day when we will see Jesus our maker. Jesus does not want you under the burden of this world. "Come unto me all ye that labor and are heavy laden and I will give you rest, take my yoke upon you and learn of me for, I am meek and lowly of heart and you will find rest for your souls. For my yoke is easy and my burden is light" (Matthew 11:28-29).

Right in the middle of this *burden* section we find the throne of grace for all who will bow before Him.

— ✧ —

Sermon 15

WATCHMAN WHAT OF THE NIGHT?
Isaiah 21:11-12

Introduction:

The office of watchman, in modern times, has almost become obsolete. This is due to the advancement of electronic detection devices in our day. In ancient times, however, the office was considered absolutely necessary for the maintenance of order and safety in towns and cities. It was the watchman's duty to watch the streets to prevent thieves and vagabonds from prowling in the dark. It was his duty to sound the alarm in case of imminent danger. It was his responsibility to warn of the approach of bad weather. Towers were erected at the entrance to cities where the watchmen were posted to scan the distant horizon for the approach of the enemy.

The watchman was a figure chosen by God to describe the role of the preacher-prophet (Ezekiel 33:1-11). It is in that sense that Isaiah uses "watchman" in our text. This strange scene takes place in Dumah, another name for Edom. While most of the nation is asleep, there are two awake. One is the watchman, God's man! The other is an Edomite, a gentile dog, a descendent of the accursed Esau. The Assyrian invasion under Sargon II has made enemies into a fellowship of fear and a brotherhood of misery. Thus, an Edomite comes to a Jewish preacher with a profound question that is eternal in its significance.

No doubt, this anxious inquirer had already found his religion lacking. In fact, the word "Dumah" used in our text means *silence*. There was no voice of comfort or hope. Heaven was silent. Then in the night one hears the cry, "Watchman, what of the night?" This question and its answer speak to every generation, but especially to this generation in which we live. Notice three things in this Scripture:

77

I. **The Anxious Question** (vs. 11)

There are five things about this question that we must take note of:

1. The question comes at an odd hour. Most people are asleep. In Israel and Edom, they are asleep while the armies of Sargon are on the move. Disaster approaches and they are asleep.

How like this age! We need an awakening. Yet, people are content to sleep while the darkness envelops us. God almighty is silent until someone awakes. Martin Luther, the great reformer said, "O my God, smite me with famine, with want, with pestilence, with all the sore diseases on earth rather than be silent to me." God will remain silent while people are willing to remain unawakened in the midst of such darkness.

2. The question comes from an odd source. It did not come from the people of God. It came from an unlikely candidate for salvation, an accursed Edomite. Oh, the glory of it! Can you see this one, spurned by religion, crying out to God's man, "What of the night?" Listen, there are people in this world crying out to the sleeping church, "What of the night?"

3. The question is well directed. It is directed to the man of God. While others are comfortable with the darkness of this world, God's man is stirred in his soul. He could not sleep with souls perishing in moral decay. He must answer the cry of the inquirer.

4. The question was important. This inquirer wanted to know how long the darkness would last. Is there a place of safety?

5. The question was an anxious question. The awakened inquirer repeats the question indicating his concern. Beloved, we live in a new dark age. It is a day when people "love the darkness," as Jesus warned. We have lived in the darkness so long we are getting accustomed to it. There are fish that live in subterranean caves that are blind. They have lived so long in the darkness they have lost their vision.

How easy it is for pulpit and pew to get in a dark rut.
How easy for us not to tend our lampstand and see our light
grow dim. How easy to forget that we are "the light of the
world."

Let a man of God sound the warning and a little light
begin to flicker and people will murmur and complain. Oh
how this world needs faithful watchmen, not hirelings. T.S.
Eliot describes it perfectly in this poem:

> The church disowned,
> The tower overthrown,
> The bells upturned -
> What have we to do
> But stand with empty hands
> And palms upturned?

In an age which moves progressively backward, God's
churches have torn down the tower and silenced the bells.
We stand with the light in our possession as the age grows
darker.

II. **The Simple Sermon** (vs. 12a)

"The morning comes and also the night."

1. The Realistic Word

Here is an ambiguous answer to the unsanctified ear. The
question asked assumed that the world was in darkness. To
the inquirer, the night was as dark as he could imagine.
His nation, family, wealth, and even life were at risk
because of the invading Assyrians. What could be worse?

No one would question this present darkness in which
we live. Jesus assumed that we would understand that
when He declared of Himself, "I am the light of the world,"
and of the church "ye are the light of the world." We live in
a new dark age. Morally our world is in blackness. Spiritually there are a few sparks of light, but most people are
asleep in the night. How we need to hear the cry of Paul in
Romans 13:11-14, "...the night is far spent, the day is at
hand, therefore let us cast off the works of darkness."

Though the present darkness is grievous, the faithful
watchman must warn of another nightfall. After the

morning there comes an even darker night. This is a clear reference to two facts:

   a. The Great Tribulation - Revelation 6:12 says of that day, "...and the sun became black as a sackcloth of hair" (See Amos 5:18-20).

   b. Hell - Matthew 8:12 and 22:13 describe Hell as a place of outer darkness. There comes a night darker than any ever experienced upon this earth!

  2. The Optimistic Word

In the midst of the midnight of this age and the darkness of the end time, there is a word of hope, "...the morning is coming." For those who know Christ there is a wonderful sunrise.

When a person is saved, it is the coming of heavenly sunrise. "For God who commanded the light to shine out of darkness has shined in our hearts to give the light of the knowledge of the glory of God in the face of Jesus Christ" (II Corinthians 4:6). Think of it, the dark night of the soul is over when Jesus comes into one's life.

Death is the believer's sunrise—it simply ushers the believer into the presence of Jesus. Paul said "...to be absent from the body is to be present with the Lord." (II Corinthians 5:8).

The rapture and resurrection speak of sunrise for the believer. Listen, beloved, the morning cometh! "Weeping may endure for the night, but joy comes in the morning" (Psalm 30:5).

Dr. W.A. Criswell was sitting on an airplane by a seminary professor. In the course of the conversation, Dr. Criswell asked about the professor's children. He noticed the man turned his face to the window and tears begin to course down his cheeks. The professor said, "I had one daughter and she died at age ten. She woke up one morning too sick to go to school. We called the doctor, and learned that she had a strange but fatal disease. In spite of all our efforts, death came in a matter of hours. A part of that affliction was gradual blindness." The dying child said, "Daddy, it's getting dark. Daddy, it's time to go to sleep. Daddy, kiss me good night. Daddy, I'll see you in the morning." The professor said, "Dr. Criswell, I am living for the morning."

> Trials dark on every hand,
>> And we cannot understand
> All the ways that God will lead us
>> To that blessed promised land.
> But He'll guide us with His eye,
>> And we'll follow till we die,
> We will understand it better by and by.

> By and By, when the morning comes,
>> When the saints of God are gathered home,
> We will tell the story, how we've overcome.
>> We will understand it better, by and by.

Conclusion:

III. **The Invitation** (vs. 12b)

"If you will inquire, inquire ye: return, come!"

1. We find here a *call to ask God.*
God is the answer to skepticism. Bring your anxious inquiries to Him.
2. Here is a *call to return.*
This is an appeal for repentance, which is the sinner returning to God.
3. Here is also a *gracious invitation to come!* God has shouted it through the ages. "Come unto me..." (Matthew 11:28). The Bible ends with God's gracious call in Revelation 22:17, "And the Spirit and the bride say, Come. And let him that heareth say, Come. And let him that is athirst come. And whosoever will, let him take the water of life freely."

Will you wake up and hear the appeal of heaven? It may be dark in your soul. You may be enveloped in the darkness of tragedy, but there is a morning coming! Don't miss it.

Some golden daybreak Jesus will come,
Some golden daybreak battles all won,
He'll shout the victory, break thru the blue,
Some golden daybreak, for me, for you.

— ✧ —

Sermon 16

HE HOLDS THE KEYS
Isaiah 22:20-25
Context, 22:1-25

Introduction:

The "valley of vision" is a synonym for Jerusalem. It is an odd designation—it would seem that the mountain top would be the place of vision. This description refers to Jerusalem as the place of God's revelation of Himself and His Word. Thus, the "valley of vision" refers to the place of privilege. More often it is in the dark valleys of life that one can see and hear from the Lord.

Something awful had happened to the people of privilege. They had heard the Word of God, but they refused to heed the Word of God. Jerusalem's inhabitants faced the danger of invasion and judgment. God had called them to repentance. What was their response? While Isaiah wept (22:4), they laughed (22:1-2). While they stored water, they forgot the God who made the water (22:11). While God calls for weeping and mourning (22:12), they responded by having a feast (22:13). Their response was, "Let us eat and drink for tomorrow we die" (22:13).

Because of this wicked and worldly response, God sentenced the nation to death (22:14). In carrying out that sentence, God began with the Prime Minister, Shebna. He was the palace steward under Ahaz, but he was stripped of that position under the reign of Hezekiah. Eliakim assumed the position and was there when God saved Judah from the Assyrian invasion under Sennacherib. This incident from Old Testament history is of extreme importance to us today for three reasons:

First, Eliakim is a type of Christ. His office pictures Jesus who is at the right hand of the Father. The Prime Minister was always at the right hand of the king.

Second, the office Eliakim prefigures the role of the

83

church to whom Christ gave the keys to the kingdom. As vice regent, Eliakim carried the keys to the locks of the king's treasures, armaments, food storage and residence.

Third, the office of Eliakim and the historical situation portrays world and church conditions at the end of the age. Revelation 3:7 says, "And to the angel of the church in Philadelphia write, 'These things says He who is holy, He who is true, He who has the key of David, He who opens and no one shuts, and shuts and no one opens.'"

Although the seven churches in Revelation 2-3 were historical churches, they illustrate churches in every age and they give a picture of the church and its condition from the days of the apostles to the end of the age. The last four churches represent the kinds of churches that will be on the earth when Christ returns. Thyatira worshiped ritual (2:25). Sardis worshiped reputation (3:3). Philadelphia worshiped Jesus (3:11). Laodicea worshiped success (3:20).

I believe our church wants to be a "Philadelphia" church. There are some who love formalism, some who love denominationalism, and some who love the trappings of success, but there are some who want to love Jesus first!

What does Isaiah 22 have to do with Revelation 2-3 and the church today? Exactly this, the conditions in Jerusalem among God's people are those that exist in the church today. Five things describe the conditions: *first*, a hunger for happiness and not holiness (22:2); *second*, a failure to face the future as God sees it (22:4-5); *third*, a refusal to repent (22:12-13); *fourth*, disregard of duty in the face of disaster (22:13); *fifth*, a love of lying leadership (22:15-19)

Shebna, stood against Isaiah, God's man, and encouraged the people in their sin. There will always be popular preachers and teachers who say what people want to hear.

God gave Judah a new leader, Eliakim, who took the keys of the kingdom. Our hope today is to look to One greater than Eliakim—Jesus Christ who holds all the keys! Of all four of the end-time churches, only one has an "open door"—the church that is listening to the One who has the keys (Revelation 3:7). In my study, God has revealed several keys on the key ring of Jesus:

I. Keys to the Kingdom - Freedom (Matthew 16:19)

Jesus has given two keys to the church. They have two different functions. One is the key of *binding the enemy.* Jesus Christ will lock up the forces that oppose His work. He has given that authority to praying Christians. The second key unlocks and *sets free those who are lost.* These keys are simply the gospel message. When Jesus died, His blood was a death blow to Satan. When He was raised, the message of life was available to all. When Jesus comes into a life, the chains fall off and that person knows real freedom. Charles Wesley wrote:

> Long my imprisoned spirit lay,
> Fast bound to sin in chains of night,
> Thine eye diffused a quickening ray,
> I awoke, my dungeon filled with light,
> The chains fell off; my heart was free;
> I arose, went forth and followed Thee.

II. Keys of Hell and Death - Future (Revelation 1:18)

Revelation 1:10-18 declares the Jesus we ought to see when the church is in the Spirit (Revelation 1:10). His voice is loud like a trumpet and the Lord has something to say to the church (Revelation 1:11). The risen Christ is shocking in His appearance. In His right hand, are the pastors of the churches. In His left hand are the keys to hell and death. His message is "Do not be afraid" (Revelation 1:17). He holds the keys to our future. Neither hell nor death can ever lock up those who belong to Jesus. The believer has a glorious future! Jesus is alive forevermore. Those of us who know the Lord have a glorious prospect.

In Tuscumbia, Alabama, there is a black pastor named Ozzie Smith. He decided to take his aging daddy anywhere he wanted to go. The old man wanted to go to Disneyland. They made the journey to California. They were the first ones in the parking lot. They got their tickets. Just before they entered, his father said, "Son, I have got to sit down." Then he collapsed. He said, "Son, I ain't never going through the gates of Disneyland, but thank God I am going through the gates of pearl." He died in his son's arms. Oh beloved, we may never see and do everything we would like here, but we have forever on the other side.

III. Key of David - Fullness

The steward carried this key on his shoulder. It opened up the residence, the treasury, the armory, and the grocery! What were the characteristics that made David different from other kings? His life was marked by *prayer* and *praise!* Keys of the kingdom bring you into the family of God. The keys of death and hell take care of your fears and future. The key of David opens up all that God has for you.

The key of praise and prayer opens up the residence of God. You "Enter His gates with thanksgiving and His courts with praise." The key opens up the treasury of God (Note Ephesians 1:6-7, 2:4, 2:7). This key opens up the armory of God. Remember, Jehoshaphat in II Chronicles 20:5-30. The enemies were invading; he did not know what to do, but his eyes were on God! He gathered the orchestra and choir and praised the beauty of holiness. When they arrived at the battleground the enemy was already defeated!

Finally, praise and prayer open up the grocery store of God! The milk, bread, and meat of God's Word are available to those who pray and praise.

Conclusion:

The Lord has the keys, and He deserves the glory. Isaiah 22:24 says prophetically of Jesus, "And they will hang on him all the glory of His Father's house." The churches that win in these last days will be those that are welcoming the glory of Jesus, and giving glory to Him.

We praise Thee, O God, for the Son of Thy love,
    For Jesus who died and is now gone above.

All glory and praise to the Lamb that was slain,
    Who has borne all our sins and has cleansed every stain.

Hallelujah, Thine the glory! Hallelujah, amen!
Hallelujah, Thine the glory! Revive us again.

—◇—

Sermon 17

THE MAJESTY OF THE MOUNTAIN
Isaiah 25:6-10

Introduction:

The great Scottish poet, Robert Burns, counted our text as his favorite Old Testament scripture. He said, "I cannot read it without weeping." The thought of a day when tears would be gone forever moved the great poet to tears!

Indeed, this passage stirs in all of us our deepest needs and hopes. There is one particular statement that ties all of these verses together, "in this mountain." Three times God makes promises that will be fulfilled on a mountain. I believe "this mountain" is clearly Calvary. How is it that God can promise to wipe away our tears? Simply because His Son had to go to "this mountain." Let us take note of some wonderful blessings He accomplished for us *In this Mountain*:

I. Souls Can Be Satisfied (25:6)

The language of verse 6 promises a life of fullness and joy. Wine is a symbol of sacrifice and celebration. When a church gathers around the table of communion with the bread and the wine, they are confessing that this world cannot satisfy. We look back to Calvary where the Lord set a table for our souls! We look forward to the "marriage supper of the Lamb." The cup of wine portrays the precious blood of Jesus Christ. When we come to the table we confess that we can praise God because of the mountain of Calvary.

II. The Dark Veil Is Vanquished (25:7)

This verse declares that there is a dark veil hanging over all people. This veil was hung over humanity by sin.

87

It is a death shroud that separates humanity from God. This veil casts a gray poll over all of life. Human happiness is always temporary, for death looms around the corner.

This veil is awful. We see in its folds all of human heartache and misery. This veil darkens life. I have seen its gray pallor lingering over children. This dark veil of sin and death washes the color out of the life of young people. This veil casts a long shadow over the life of adults.

This veil is best understood when one remembers two Old Testament pictures. One, Moses had to veil his face because it shone with the glory of God when he returned from Mt. Sinai. The people could only see a glimmer of God's glory.

In the tabernacle and later the temple, God hung a heavy veil between the Holy place and the Holy of Holies. No person could go behind that veil except the high priest, once a year, and then not without blood. The veil said to all of humanity, "Keep out, you cannot get to God." If you were a Gentile, you were four courts away from even seeing the veil. If you were a Jewish woman, you were three courts away. If you were a Jewish male, you were still two courts away. If you were a priest you could see the veil, but you could not go in unless you were the high priest. Man was separated from God.

Look at the promise in our text. "He will destroy in this mountain...the veil" (25:7). Did this happen? Look at Matthew 27:51, "And behold the veil of the temple was rent in twain from top to the bottom and the earth did quake and the rocks were rent." In that moment everything that hung between man and God was torn down so that now people of faith can go directly to the throne of God. When the veil was torn, God transferred the Holy of Holies, His throne on the earth, to Mt. Calvary, and from there to the hearts of all who believed.

In Luke 23:45, the same incident about the veil is reported just after Jesus said to a dying thief, a sinner, "Today you can go with me to Paradise." In Mark 15:78 after the veil is torn down, immediately a Roman centurion, a Gentile, confesses Christ as the Son of God (Read Ephesians 2:11-18). Think of it; our Lord tore down the wall, the veil that hung between man and God. Hebrews 6:20 says that this wonderful truth is "anchor of our souls." In Hebrews 10:19-22, we read this remarkable invitation, "Having therefore brethren boldness to enter into the holiest by the blood of Jesus, by a new and living way which He hath consecrated for us through the veil, that is to say His flesh, and having a high priest over the house of God; Let us draw near with a true heart and in full assurance of faith."

Beloved, we can get to the Father, to the feast, and to a glorious future because on "this mountain" our Lord tore away the veil of sin, death and separation.

> Down at the Cross, where my Savior died,
> Down where for cleansing from sin I cried,
> There to my heart was the blood applied,
> Glory to His name.

III. **Death Is Destroyed** (25:8)

This wonderful verse is quoted by Paul in the great resurrection chapter of I Corinthians 15:54. Jesus Christ faced death in its own territory. He went to "this mountain" to die for the sins of the world. Hell did its worst. Man's depravity was at its lowest. Religion was viciously murderous. Politics was at its all time low. The perfect man was hatefully slain on a cross. His spirit descended into the dark vaults of the dead. He announced to the waiting sons in paradise, pack up, in three days I'll be back to carry you home. He then descended into the realm of the damned and announced doom upon Satan and the armies of hell. Three days later He came out of the grave with the keys to hell and death. He swallowed the sting of death. He renounced the fear of death. He destroyed the power of death. He destroyed the authority of death, Satan himself.

Remember that in Pharaoh's court when Moses' rod became a serpent, Pharaoh's magician turned their rods into serpents. Then Moses' rod swallowed their's! Our Lord has swallowed up all of death for us. Later Pharaoh's army was "swallowed by the Red Sea." Our ancient enemies have been defeated.

IV. **Tears Are Taken Away** (25:8b)

This very phrase is quoted in Revelation 21:4. This verse speaks of our present day and the promised day. Right now God is the God of all comfort. It is His nailed pierced hand that alone can stroke the tears of sorrow from our faces.

When I go to "this mountain" and see what He has endured for me, my sorrows are so much less. See the tears on His face as He weeps over a city, over Lazarus' at his tomb, and in Gethsemane! Hebrews 5:7 says, "who in the days of His flesh offered up prayers and supplication with strong crying and tears..." Our Lord was a man of sorrows. He shed tears so that our's might one day be vanquished.

V. **There Is Deliverance from Disgrace** (25:8c)

Just a word about this promise. Sin is a shameful thing. Where on this earth can a person find full and free forgiveness? Where is there cleansing and acceptance. If a person of prominence falls into sin and disgrace, the press will crucify him. Often, society will shun him. Even the church may refuse to restore him. At Calvary (this mountain), all disgrace is removed. Jesus' precious blood covers our sins. No wonder Paul, who murdered Stephen and blasphemed Christ, could say after he had been to Calvary, "I am not ashamed of the gospel of Christ, for it is the power of God to salvation" (Romans 1:16).

> Amazing grace, How sweet the sound,
> That saved a wretch like me.
> I once was lost, but now I am found
> Was blind but now I see.

VI. **Hope Is Heralded** (25:9)

Perhaps these verses are a reference to the people waiting for the Lord during the Assyrian invasion. The angel of the Lord destroyed the Assyrian army as the people waited and prayed. Our hope is in what God can do, not in our own works.

Always, our world has waited for God. Israel awaited

the birth of the Messiah and yet missed Him. The world now awaits the second coming of Jesus Christ. Because He died on the cross and I have trusted Him, I can now wait in joy for that moment when He returns. Others of you are still waiting to be saved. You have searched for hope in all that the world has to offer and have found it trite, trivial, and temporary. Your hungry heart awaits the entrance of the King. You can receive Him today and "be glad and rejoice in His salvation."

VII. **Our Enemy Is Eliminated** (25:10-12)

Calvary crushed Satan, disarmed the demonic, and made it possible to live in victory. Notice that the enemy is trodden under foot. This is what Jesus did to Satan. Psalm 110 had predicted that our Lord's enemies would be put under His feet. Ephesians 1:22 says, "And hath put all things under His feet..." Romans 16:20 says, "and the God of peace will bruise Satan under your feet shortly..." What Jesus did on "this mountain" placed our enemy under subjection to us.

Our enemy has been "spoiled" (28:11). Colossians 2:15 says, "and having spoiled principality and powers he made a show of them openly triumphing over them in it." At Calvary, our Lord slapped the demons in the face and publicly defeated them.

Finally, our Lord has torn down the walls of the "fortresses" and strongholds of Satan (25:12) (II Corinthians 10:4).

Conclusion:

Oh, what our Lord has done for us on "this mountain" called Calvary. I remember well the dear lady named Mrs. Waites. She was dying of cancer. We had prayed for her healing. God was choosing to take her. I visited in her home. It was a modest country home with board walls, a pump instead of faucets, and a pot bellied stove. As I tried to offer her sympathy she said, "Young pastor, don't worry about me. My Lord suffered so much more for me on Calvary. I love Him, and I am satisfied with Jesus. He is enough."

Have you ever been to "this mountain" called Calvary?
It is only there that your soul can really be satisfied.

> I am satisfied with Jesus;
>   He has done so much for me.
> He has suffered to redeem me;
>   He has died to set me free.
>
> I am satisfied, I am satisfied,
>   I am satisfied with Jesus.
> But the question comes to me,
>   As I think of Calvary,
> Is my master satisfied with me?

PEACE IN A STORM TOSSED WORLD
Isaiah 26:1-12

Introduction:

J.A. Alexander believes that this song was inspired after God's miraculous deliverance of Jerusalem from the Assyrian army under Sennacherib. According to Assyrian sources, Sennacherib boasted of his siege of Jerusalem, "I have shut up Hezekiah like a bird in a cage." Hezekiah prayed and God sent one angel who slew one hundred eighty-five thousand Assyrian soldiers (37:36). Later, as Sennacherib worshiped a false God named Nisroch, he was assassinated by two of his sons.

As Judah celebrated this temporal victory, they looked forward to the ultimate triumph of God. They celebrated the practical and prophetical benefits given them by the God of their salvation.

The truth is that everything we look forward to in heaven is our's now in a practical and spiritual way. We live in a world of conflict. The political arena of our world is one of conflict. From Washington to London to Lithuania the cry is for peace. Our families lack peace. One-half our marriages end in divorce and husband-wife, parent-child conflicts are at an all time high. Fifty percent of the homicides in America are domestic. Individual lives are filled with conflict. The answer to this conflict is God's peace. Just as God's victory over the Assyrian army gave Jerusalem peace, so God can overthrow every enemy of peace in your life.

The word "peace" translates the Hebrew word *shalom*. This word occurs two hundred fifty times in two hundred thirteen separate verses of the Old Testament. This word means much more than absence of war and strife. It means completeness, wholeness, harmony on the inside, unimpaired relationships. It is the word used by both Jew and

Arab as a greeting. The Jew greets with *shalom* and the Arab with *salam*.

In our text, we find the expression "perfect peace." Literally, it is in the Hebrew "in peace, peace." The idea is of an inexpressible peace. The promise of peace comes only to those who cease their rebellion, lay down their weapons, and bow at the feet of Jesus Christ. When that happens, a person has peace with God. Then the benefits of peace can flow. Our text teaches three wonderful aspects of peace with God:

I. The Community of Peace (26:1-2)

In the midst of a world in conflict, God has provided a sanctuary, a place of peace. I believe that God's ancient people, Israel, were to enjoy that kind of a community. In our day, the church is the community of peace. We are at war with the devil, but at peace with each other. We are on a collision course with the world's agenda, but we have a confident serenity in our hearts. Let's consider a three-fold description of the community of peace:

1. A Singing Community (vs. 1)
They have something to sing about. God has defeated their enemies and saved them. There is joy in the community of faith.

2. A Secure Community (vs. 1)
The walls of this city are salvation. We live in the secure borders appointed by our Lord. Salvation's walls are around all who repent of their sin, believe the gospel, and receive Christ as Lord.

3. A Seeking Community (vs. 2)
The gates of this community are open to all who will obey the truth. The church is not a closed shop, but an open door.

Yet, in our individualistic and self-centered day, people have little use for the church. Bible study and music can be had via radio, television, tape, or conference. No one wants the responsibilities that accompany real community. Some of you are sitting in a class when you need to be feeding others. You choose a church on the basis of what its ministries can do for you. Have you asked, "What can God do through me for His church?"

Dr. D. James Kennedy has said, "Most people think of a church as a drama, with the minister as the chief actor, God as the prompter, and the laity as the critic. What is actually the case is that the congregation is the chief actor, the minister the prompter, and God the critic."

What do you look for in a church? You should ask, "Is Jesus Christ there?" "Is He loved there?" "Does God want me there?" If He is there, it will be a community of peace.

A room of praise, a temple of peace,
    A home of faith where doubtings cease,
A house of comfort where hope is given,
    A source of strength to help us to heaven,
A place of worship, a place to pray,
    I found all this in my church today.

- O.W. Glassburn

II. **The Covenant of Peace** (26:3-4)

Peace is the gift of God and the heritage of all who know Him. In two-thirds of its uses in scripture, the word "peace" is associated with the presence of the Lord. Isaiah 54:10 speaks of God's covenant of peace.

1. The Foundation of Peace
In our text, we find the double mention of the covenant name of God, Yahweh. This is the name by which God entered into covenant with Israel through Moses. This name means "I Am."

The idea that peace comes from God, is a gift from God, and flows from a knowledge of His presence is Biblical.

The idea of a covenant-making, covenant-keeping God is unique to the Bible. When a covenant was made in Israel, an animal was slain and divided. The two parties making covenant passed through the bloody remains of the divided animal pledging their lives for the agreement. Even so, God ratified His covenant of peace at the cross (Read Colossians 1:20-21). When you came to the cross, you made peace with God.

Human covenants of peace have never remained. From

1500 B.C. to the present, more than ten thousand treaties of peace have been recorded. The average length of those treaties remaining in force is two years. Thank God, our covenant with Christ is permanent.

2. The Focus of Peace

It is one thing to receive peace, it is quite another to abide in peace. Our text gives the secret of living in serenity and peace of mind. Notice the phrase, "whose mind is stayed on thee." Literally, the Hebrew reads, "whose steadfast purpose is God." Yahweh is the great "I Am." The believer lives in peace when his heart and mind are focused on who God is! Whatever you need, God says, "I Am."

In John 14:27, Jesus said, "Peace I leave with you, my peace I give unto you: not as the world giveth, give I unto you. Let not your heart be troubled, neither let it be afraid." This promise is found in the gospel of John, a book filled with Jesus declaring that He is the great "I Am." He said, "I am the bread of life, the light of the world, the water of life, and the resurrection and the life, to name a few things. Peace is possible when our mind is focused on Christ.

Philippians 4:4-9 gives the wonderful explanation of Isaiah 26:3-4. We are to rejoice in the Lord, praising Him for who He is. We are to request of the Lord. Finally, we are to rest in the Lord. God's peace "keeps" (same word as Isaiah) or stands guard over our hearts and minds. Then as we think on the things of God, Paul says, "The God of peace shall be with you."

> Peace, peace, wonderful peace,
> Coming down from the Father above,
> Sweep over my spirit forever I pray,
> In fathomless billows of love.

3. The Faith that Brings Peace (vs. 3-4)

Two times we are told in these verses to "trust the Lord." Faith is believing that God will do what He says. "Trust" in Hebrew means to lean your whole weight upon. Faith is resting your whole life on the word of God. In verse 4, the phrase "everlasting strength" translates the Hebrew phrase, "everlasting Rock" or "Rock of the ages." When you put your faith in Jesus, you are standing on the solid Rock.

My hope is built on nothing less,
    Than Jesus' blood and righteousness;
I dare not trust the sweetest frame,
    But wholly lean on Jesus' name.

His oath, His covenant, His blood,
    Support me in the whelming flood;
When all around my soul gives way,
    He then is all my hope and stay.

When darkness seems to hide His face,
    I rest on His unchanging grace;
In every high and stormy gale,
    My anchor holds within the veil.

On Christ, the solid Rock, I stand,
    All other ground is sinking sand.

                                - Edward Mote

I'm standing on the Rock of ages,
    Safe from all the storm that rages;
Rich, but not from Satan's wages;
    I'm standing on the solid Rock.

                                - Harold Lane

III. **The Choice of Peace** (26:5-12)

We cannot always choose our outward circumstances, but we can choose to live at peace with God, ourselves, and those in the family. Let me just briefly mention what God's peace does not do in this temporal world:

1.   It does not remove you from a world of conflict (5-6). We will experience conflict with the world, the flesh, and the devil as long as we live.

2.   It does not guarantee immediate solution to problems. We are counseled to "wait on the Lord" (vs. 8).

3.   It does not promise life without difficulty. Verse 9 indicates that the believer desires the Lord "in the night." Dark shadows fall across all our lives.

4.   It will not remove you from contact with the wicked (vs. 10). However, we can choose to walk with the Lord in this world. We can choose to "wait on the Lord" rather than fret. We can choose to worship the Lord and desire Him more than this world. We can choose to work in His strength and not our own (vs. 12). This is the secret of peace:

> Walking in His victory,
> Waiting in His hope,
> Worshiping in His love,
> Working in His strength.

Conclusion:

High in the Andes mountains on the border of Argentina and Chile is an interesting sculpture made of old cannons, the weapons of war. For years, these two nations fought over the location of the border. Finally, in 1903 the boundary was agreed upon. Senora de Costia had the monument erected. It is a statue of Christ, known as the "Christ of the Andes." On its base, are these words, "Sooner shall these mountains crumble into dust than Argentines and Chileans break the peace sworn at the feet of Christ the Redeemer." Thank God for the day at the feet of Christ when the Redeemer, God spoke everlasting peace between my soul and heaven. The Negro spiritual song says,

> Gonna lay down my burden,
> Down by the riverside,
> Down by the riverside.
> Gonna lay down my burden,
> Down by the riverside,
> Gonna study war no more,
> Ain't gonna study war no more!

When you come to the river of Calvary, you can lay down your burden. War with God is over. Peace is your eternal legacy.

— ✧ —

THE DEAD SHALL LIVE
Isaiah 26:18-27:1

Introduction:

A strange incident took place early in my ministry. A couple in our church told me they were expecting a child. All the usual things a country church does for an expectant mother were done. Showers were held and advice given to the expectant mother. She began to grow and display all the physical signs of pregnancy. The end of her term drew near, and she finally decided to go to the doctor. The doctor reported that there was no baby! She had a rare problem that occurred in women who desire to have a baby. She had a false pregnancy. Her body had all the signs of childbearing, but there was no life there.

In verses 17-18 of our text, God compares the people to a woman with all the pangs of childbirth, but gives birth only to wind. All human efforts to get out of this world alive are futile. Every year sixty million people die.

The new age movement with its Hindu theology of reincarnation views death as a friend. The Bible views death as an enemy, the result of man's fall into sin, and the sad climax to all human achievement.

Our text sets forth the only hope people have in the face of the certainty of death. We should live life under God to its fullest, yet the inevitability of death stalks all of humanity. It is the promise of life beyond death that gives strength. What man cannot accomplish God has done for us. Look at three wonderful aspects of the resurrection:

I. **The Hope of the Resurrection** (26:19a)

This verse declares a wonderful promise, "thy dead shall live." This hope was not clearly understood in ancient times. In the Old Testament there are few direct references to life after death as resurrection. Resurrection means more than eternal life. It means living for eternity in a body like the body of Jesus Christ.

The ancient societies believed in life after death. The Greeks believed, as did the Romans—that the soul lived on outside the body. The Egyptians believed in resurrection, for they sought to preserve the bodies of the dead as mummies. Elaborate graves were made and filled with things to be used after the resurrection.

The Jews believed that there was an existence as a soul or shadow. In a few places in the Old Testament, the light breaks through. Abraham's willingness to offer Isaac is a clear picture of belief in the resurrection. Joseph's desire to have his body removed from Egypt to Israel indicates a similar belief. Job cries out in his despair, "I know that my redeemer liveth, and in the latter day shall stand upon the earth, and though worms destroy this body, yet in my flesh I shall see God" (Job 19:25-26). That ancient hope and promise was answered by the death and resurrection of Jesus Christ.

As we look at the human body, we can feel the same despair. A person may, as Job, see a body ravaged by disease. One may see his body changed by age. Others see birth defects and damage caused by accidents. Yet as we view our dying bodies, we have hope, "Thy dead shall live...they shall arise."

A former associate pastor at First Baptist Church of Dallas, Gary Holder, led a man, named Bill, to Christ. Bill's family, wife and seven children, had ridden to church on a bus. Finally, on the associate's last Sunday, Bill accepted Christ as his personal Savior. The associate moved on to his own pastorate. One day Bill called to tell him that his wife had terminal cancer and had been given six months to live. She wanted Bro. Holder to preach her funeral. Six months later she died. Bro. Holder arrived just in time for the services. There stood that daddy with three children hanging on each leg and one in his arms, standing over mamma's casket. Bill said, "Bro. Holder, I've been to the bottom and I know Jesus is alive, and He is enough to get us through."

II. The Hallelujah of the Resurrection (26:19b)

"Awake and sing ye that dwell in the dust" (26:19). In Genesis 3:19, the awful curse came upon every son of Adam. "In the sweat of thy face shalt thou eat bread, till thou return unto the ground; for out of it were thou taken: for dust thou art and unto dust thou shall return." Satan was sentenced to dwell in the dust as well, "...upon thy belly shalt thou go and dust shalt thou eat all the days of thy life" (Genesis 3:14).

These words in Micah 7:17 describe those who reject God. "They shall lick the dust like a serpent, they shall move out of their holes like worms of the earth, they shall be afraid of the Lord our God, and shall fear because of thee."

Abraham confessed that he was but "dust and ashes" (Genesis 4:27). Job repented in "dust and ashes" (Job 42:6). In Psalm 22, we have a remarkable prophesy and description of our Lord's death. Psalm 22:1 begins with the cry "My God, my God, why hast thou forsaken me." Then look at what our Lord endured in verses 14-17 of Psalm 22. This phrase sums it up, "...thou hast brought me unto the dust of death" (Psalm 22:15). You see, our Lord saw what we were. He saw us as earthbound, created out of dust, condemned to a dusty grave, harassed by a serpent cursed to the dust, and He was willing to be brought unto the dust of death. Psalm 103:10-14 describes the forgiving power of our Lord who tasted the dust of our death. "He remembereth that we are but dust" (Psalm 103:14). David cried out in Psalm 30:9 "...shall the dust praise thee?" Daniel 12:2 answers, "and many that sleep in the dust of the earth shall awake, some to everlasting life and some to everlasting shame and contempt."

Our text says it clearly, "Awake and sing you that dwell in the dust" (26:19). Our Lord has given the dust dwellers life and hope. When they laid our Lord in the tomb, all the hopes of the ages were buried. When they buried our Lord the dust muffled the music of heaven. On the third day, the angel moved the stone and said to the stone, "Hallelujah, He is risen." The stone rolled against a tree and rumbled,

"Hallelujah, He is risen." The tree shook its limbs and whispered to the branches, "Hallelujah, He is risen." The branches brushed against the birds and clapped their leaves together saying, "Hallelujah, He is risen." The birds soared into the sky and whistled, "Hallelujah, He is risen." The angels in glory heard it and bowed their heads in wonder and said, "Hallelujah, He is risen." One day when I was living in the dust of death, the Holy Spirit spoke to my heart and said, "Hallelujah, He is risen." Then the angels of God beheld my heart, as I was born again, and said, "Hallelujah, Ron Phillips is now risen." "And you hath He raised who were dead in trespasses and sin" (Ephesians 2:1). One glad day we shall rise to meet Him in the air at His coming. Yes, because He lives, even the dust can sing praises to His name.

> We shall rise, Hallelujah
> We shall rise, Amen!
> In that resurrection morning
> When the dead in Christ shall rise,
> We shall rise, we shall rise!

III. **The Harvest of the Resurrection** (26:19c - 27:1)

"For thy dew is as the dew herbs, and the earth shall cast out her dead" (26:19). This image is of a harvest that comes when the dew falls on the dusty ground. Just as the plants grow, the earth will cast up the dead. This image is consistent with New Testament truth. Jesus described His own death as a seed cast into the ground. "Most assuredly I say unto you, unless a grain of wheat falls into the ground and dies, it remains alone; but if it dies it produces much grain" (John 12:24). A few verses later Jesus said, "And I, if I am lifted up from the earth, will draw all peoples to myself."

You see, Jesus Christ's resurrection guarantees our resurrection. First Corinthians 15:20-26 describes the resurrection harvest. "Christ, the firstfruits, afterward, those that are Christ's at His coming, then comes the end when He has delivered the Kingdom to God the Father, when He puts an end to all rule, authority, and power. For

He must reign till He has put all enemies under His feet. The last enemy that will be destroyed is death."

Our Lord's life was cast into the ground, but on the third day, heavenly dew began to fall and the seed He had planted began to blossom until, at last, out of His grave came the Rose of Sharon and the Lily of the Valley!

Oh, beloved, the dew is an emblem of the Holy Spirit. The heavenly life-giving dew is available today. On this special day, if you have been away from God, listen to His promise. "I will heal their backsliding, I will love them freely for my anger has turned away from Him. I will be like the dew to Israel, he shall grow like the lily" (Hosea 14:4-5).

Think on this, you and I can be like the lily of the valley! Heavenly dew is falling today to bring life to those who dwell in the dust. You can be a part of the harvest. One day Jesus will come for us. First Thessalonians 4:16 says, "The Lord Himself will descend from heaven with a shout, the voice of the archangel, and with the trumpet of God and the dead in Christ shall rise first, then we which are alive and remain shall be caught up together with them in the cloud, to meet our Lord in the air..."

Isaiah 26:20-21 gives us the words of His shout, "Come my people, enter your chamber and shut your doors...For behold the Lord comes out of His place to punish the inhabitants of the earth."

One day Jesus will gather the final harvest of those who belong to Him. The earth will receive its harvest of Judgment, and Satan will receive his final blow from God's sword (27:1). Those of us upon whom the heavenly dew has come will be safe with Jesus.

Conclusion:

When I was in High School, I had a friend who really had a crush on the girl who later became my wife. When I was not around, he would not let anyone bother her. I went to college; he went to Vietnam. Word came back that Melvin had been killed. I was preaching in my hometown on Easter Sunday morning at a little church that had no pastor. I stood up to preach, and sitting in the back of the building was a soldier who looked like Melvin. I stumbled through the message, gave the invitation, and the soldier boy walked down the aisle. It was Melvin! There had been a mixup. He had been wounded, but he was alive. That morning he gave his heart to Jesus. He was back from the dead—not only from war, but from spiritual death! If you are not a Christian, you need life now and life after death—Heaven with Christ.

— ✧ —

Sermon 20

CHRIST THE CORNERSTONE
Isaiah 28:1-20

Introduction:

Ephraim became the most prominent tribe among the tribes of Israel that made up the Northern Kingdom. Ephraim's capitol was the lovely city of Samaria. Archaeologist tell us that this city graced a beautiful hill. It looked as if the city was a crown of beauty for the top of that hill, but this outward glitz and glitter covered a corrupt and decaying society.

In every generation, societies built upon human pride and achievement are destined to fail. For Ephraim, the marks of failure hidden under the facade of progress were as follows: pride, drunkenness, rejection of God's glory, and corrupt ministry.

How sad that people would rather wear the crown of human pride rather than God's crown of glory. You can either have your pride or His presence. You cannot have both. Israel refused to speak God's word in their language, accepting, instead of spiritual food, the world's vomit (28:7-10). Therefore, God promised that He would one day speak His word to them in the tongues of foreign nations. (This is a prophecy of Pentecost and the real purpose of the gift of tongues. See I Corinthians 14:20-25. Tongues were a sign to the Jew, who had rejected God's revelation, that God had indeed spoken in Christ.)

Let us take warning from this historical incident. Upon what values are our lives built? What are the bedrock foundational truths upon which your life stands? What about your family, the church, our nation? Have we rejected the word of God and the God of the Word for humanism? Have we become a nation of addicts and drunkards? Are we satisfied with spiritual food that looks good, but is in reality vomit! Have we made an agreement with death and hell?

105

This scripture speaks of the true foundation for life at its best. There is a place to rest your life. There is One upon whose life you can build your life. He is described in our text as a stone.

I.   The Identity of the Stone

This Stone prophesied here is none other than Jesus Christ. There are at least eight references to this text found in the New Testament, all of which point to Christ as the Stone. Among those texts is I Peter 2:6-8. In that passage, we find Isaiah 28:16, Psalm 118:22, and Isaiah 8:14 quoted in reference to Jesus. He is the chief Stone, the rejected Stone, and the offensive Stone!

II.   The Ability of the Stone

"A tried Stone" The word "tried" means *put to the test and proven*. It was used of metal being tried by the fires of the refiner. Our Lord Jesus has been "tried" in every realm. He was tested by the Father who reported, "This is my beloved Son." He was tried by Satan who offered Him all the kingdoms of this world. Jesus gained the victory over Satan. He said, "The prince of this world cometh, and has nothing in me" (John 14:30). Demons unsuccessfully attacked Jesus. He was tried by nature. The stormy winds fell silent and rustled harmlessly away at His word. The ocean waves laid down for a nap at His word. The fish crawled into a net to honor His command. Jesus was "tried" by men. He was never confounded by a question of man, never overwhelmed by a problem, and never met a need He could not meet.

He was tried in life and no one ever lived as He did. He was tried in death and suffered its worst without complaint. Death could not hold the Son of God. He was tried in eternity and given a name which is above every name. Jesus was tried with our trials and never tried in vain. Recently, a person told me the reason he had never been saved. It seems that some Christian had disappointed him. My response to that person was simple. Go home and write down everything you have seen Christians do that has turned you away. Then write the name of Jesus on another sheet of paper and write everything He has done to disappoint you. Then decide if you want to go to hell because others have failed, or go to Heaven because of Jesus who never fails. He has been tried and never found wanting.

III. The Stability of the Stone

Jesus is called a precious cornerstone. Now a cornerstone served several functions, but its main function was to unify. The strongest stones were always placed at the corners of those ancient structures. These stones supported and tied the building together. Jesus is the One who ties everything together.

1. He alone ties the Godhead together, for "in Him dwells all the fullness of the Godhead bodily" (Colossians 2:9).

2. Jesus alone holds the creation together (Colossians 1:16-17).

3. Jesus holds the Bible together. If you take Jesus out of the Bible, there is no unity. He ties the Testaments together.

4. Jesus holds the church together. He is the Head of the church, the owner of the church, the lover of the church and the builder of the church!

5. Jesus is the only One who can put your life together! If Jesus is not at the center of your life, sooner or later it will fall apart.

IV. The Rarity of the Stone

Christ is called "precious" in our text. That word means valuable. There is no one who is the peer of Jesus. There is no one like Him.

> Lord, you are more precious than silver.
> Lord, you are more costly than gold.
> Lord, you are more beautiful than diamonds.
> Nothing I desire compares to Thee.

> Precious name, oh how sweet,
> Hope of earth and joy of Heaven.

> Precious name, oh how sweet,
> Hope of earth and joy of Heaven.

No sacrifice for Him is too great. Whatever you may think it will cost you to become a Christian, it will be worth it!

Conclusion:

There is a warning and a promise in the passage. In verse 20 some are like a tall person who is sleeping in a short bed. No matter how he tries, he cannot get comfortable. No matter how he tugs, the cold winds still find part of his body uncovered. How like life this is. All human efforts at lasting joy are futile. There is never quite enough to satisfy.

Yet Jesus has "covered" (28:18 - literal translation) our covenant in His death. Jesus can cover our *debts*, our *deeds* and our *difficulties*. What is the requirement to the believer? "Whoever believes will not act hastily" (28:16). It means if you believe you will not rush away from Jesus. You will come to Him for all of life.

— ✧ —

CHRIST THE ROCK OF AGES
Isaiah 32:1-20

Introduction:

Anyone who has traveled to the middle east knows that Israel is a land of rocks and stones. Even in the fields they must plow around the rocks. Rocks and stones were the building materials of that day. The ancient ruins are rocks and stones.

For this reason, the terms *rock and stone* are figures of speech throughout the word of God. Among the similes and metaphors, the most glorious is the Rock of Ages, the Lord Jesus Christ. Throughout the Scriptures, He is described as a rock. Isaiah 32:2 says, "And a man shall be as a hiding place from the wind, and a cover from the tempest; as a river of water in a dry place, as a shadow of a great rock in a weary land." In this great prophecy, we see that a man will be like the protection of a great rock overshadowing us.

In these messages, we shall learn about our Lord Jesus as the Rock of the ages. In this message, we shall examine how He is the Rock in our experience of salvation; and the Rock in our Christian life.

I. Christ the Smitten Rock
(Exodus 17:6, I Corinthians 10:4)

In Exodus 17, we have the account of the children of Israel in the wilderness. There is no water, so they chide Moses about the lack. Moses is commanded to smite the rock. After the rock is smitten, water flows from it. This rock is a beautiful picture of Christ. He was smitten that the water of life might flow out to sinners. First Corinthians 10:4 confirms this picture, "for they drank of that spiritual Rock that followed them and that Rock was Christ." Later, Moses missed the promised land because he struck the rock a second time. His mistake spoiled the picture, for Christ was "once offered" for our sins. He is not to be crucified again. Moses should have spoken to the rock.

This is what we must do today. We are to ask the Rock for the water of life. And when we come by faith and ask Jesus, He will save us. When our Lord went to the cross, it was there that the Rock of ages was smitten. From His wounded side came forth water and blood. Blood was shed for our cleansing and water for the giving of life. Christ suffered for our sins that we might have life.

After the Civil War, General Gordon was up for nomination for a political position. One of the men on the committee who had served with him did not like the General. When the general came in and the man saw him, he changed his vote to a vote for the General. When asked why he changed he said, "When I saw the scars on the general's face, I could not vote against him." When you and I see the scars on the smitten Son of God, how can we not cast our all before Him.

II. **Christ the Saving Rock**

Moses called Him the rock of creation and salvation (Deuteronomy 32:15, 18). David cried in Psalm 89:26, "Thou art my Father, my God, and the Rock of my salvation." Also in Psalm 95:1, we are called upon to "make a joyful noise to the Rock of our salvation."

Salvation is pictured in these passages as deliverance and protection. To be saved is to be safe. The picture is one where enemies are defeated and destroyed, and the saved person has been brought to a place of safety. This is exactly what Jesus Christ has done for us. He has routed our enemies and brought us to a place of safety.

III. **Christ the Sheltering Rock**

Christ is not only our Savior, He is our shelter. We are now hidden in the Rock. We are in the "shadow of that great rock, in a weary land" (32:2). Psalm 94:22 says, "But the Lord is my defense and my God is the rock of my refuge."

Once we are saved, we are in Christ. We are safe

within the Rock of ages. We have His protection and watchcare over us. What assurance this is for us.

Once, during the wars between Spain and France, the Spanish sent a note to the French commander, General Colingy, saying, "Surrender, we are more numerous than you." The general wrote a note, fastened it to an arrow and shot it into the Spanish camp. It read, "Surrender? Never! We have our king with us." When we are tempted to give up, when we are battling doubt and discouragement, we must remember that our King is with us. We are under His protection.

> Rock of Ages, cleft for me,
> Let me hide myself in Thee.

IV. Christ the Scorned Rock

The Lord Jesus is indeed the Rock of salvation. Through the ages, there have been countless multitudes who would not receive Him. Psalm 118:22 says, "The stone which the builders refused has become the head of the corner." Jesus was rejected by the experts, the Jews. Yet, He has become the head stone and cornerstone. Paul confirms that Jesus has become a stumbling stone on the road to hell instead of a stepping stone to heaven (Romans 9:32-33). The Jews stumbled because salvation is by faith, not works. The Greeks stumbled over its simplicity.

Jesus Christ, the Rock of ages, may still be a scorned stone. He may still be a stumbling stone. Sadly, Jesus Himself cited Psalm 118:22 in Matthew 21:42-44. After quoting those words, He issued a dire warning. "And whosoever shall fall on this stone shall be broken: but on whomsoever it shall fall, it will grind him to powder" (Matthew 21:44). Fall on that Rock today and be broken before God. If you are not in the Rock, the Rock shall one day fall upon you in judgment.

V. Christ the Solid Rock
(Matthew 16:18, I Corinthians 3:11)

For us who are saved and a part of the church, there is solid ground under our feet. Our lives are built upon a secure foundation. Jesus said in Matthew 16:18, "Upon this rock I will build my church." This reference is not to Peter but to the content of Peter's confession. The rock-bed of essential truth is the person of Christ. First Corinthians 3:11 assures us, "For other foundations can no man lay than that which is laid, which is Jesus Christ." He is the support and solidarity that undergirds us. Jesus told a parable about two house builders. One built upon the shifting sand and another upon the rock. The storms blew down the house upon the sand, but the house upon the rock stood. It was a parable of life. We may build our lives upon the faulty philosophies and the shifting sands of this world, but suddenly, adversity, disappointment or defeat will descend in tornadoes of trouble and cyclones of confusion. The life that you tried to build without Christ will not stand.

By the end of this decade, suicide may very well be the number one killer in America. Already, it is the number one killer of youth. We cannot build our lives on materialism, pleasure seeking, fame, or fortune. All these are "will of the wisp." Take Freddy Prinze who had everything but what he needed and became a victim of suicide. Not all of the fame of Steve McQueen nor all of his fortune could drive away the cancer that claimed his life. Oh how our lives should be built on the eternal Rock of Ages.

> His oath, His covenant, His blood,
> Support me in the whelming flood.
> When all around my soul gives way
> He then is all my hope and stay.

> On Christ the solid Rock I stand,
> All other ground is sinking sand.

VI. Christ the Supplying Rock
(Exodus 17:6, I Corinthians 10:4)

Let's return to that Rock in the wilderness. It was a picture of Christ. After it was smitten, one simply had to speak to the Rock to get water. Christ continues to be the total supply for those who have trusted Him.

He is our never failing supply of spiritual refreshment

in the wilderness of this world. First Corinthians 10:4 states, "They all drank of the same spiritual drink, for they drank of that spiritual Rock that went with them, and that Rock was Christ." Notice, the source was with them. They all shared in the abundant supply. It would seem that each got all he wanted. Furthermore, if a man did not come to the Rock, he would not get any refreshment. Those who witness are like a man with a bucket of cold water going to a desert place. He says to the thirsty, here is a little water but let me take you to the fountain. How we need to bring people to the Rock of supply. Are you sin-sick and dry of soul and spirit? Is your spiritual life parched and barren? He is the source of refreshing supply.

> All the way my Savior leads me.
>> Cheers each winding path I tread,
> Gives me grace for every trial,
>> Feeds me with the living bread.
> Though my weary steps may falter
> And my soul athirst may be
> Gushing from the Rock before me,
>> Lo a spring of joy I see.

VII. Christ the Sweetening Rock (Psalm 81:16)

"And with honey out of the Rock should I have satisfied thee." In the mountains of Israel the bees would build large hives. Often, these hives were remote. When discovered, they would be so full of honey that it would be oozing a long way down the rocks. This was why it was called a "land flowing with milk and honey." Honey was the natural sweetener of the day.

In this symbolic picture, Jesus the Rock is giving forth sweetness. He is the great life-sweetener. There are some experiences in life that are tragic and often bitter. Somehow in the midst of all the anger, frustration, and bitterness, we find Jesus. We can look back upon our brief life and see not a year without difficulty. Thank God, though, there was not a year without Jesus.

> Jesus is the sweetest name I know,
>> And He's just the same, as His lovely name;
> And that's the reason why I love Him so,
>> Jesus is the sweetest name I know.

VIII. Christ the Supreme Rock
(I Peter 2:4-8, Daniel 2:34)

When our lives are over; when this planet revolves for the last time; when the world explodes in fire to be remade; when it is all over, Christ will still be the Rock of the ages. Thank God, He is Rock of the past ages, the present age, and the age to come.

Daniel 2:34, 44-45 gives us the dream of Nebuchadnezzar. In the dream, a Stone is cut, without hands, out of a mountain. This Stone crushed the kingdom of this earth, "and it shall stand forever." This is the kingdom of the Son of God. He is the Stone cut without hands that will come to fulfill the promises and establish a new earth with a new kingdom.

> I'm building on the Rock,
>> Upon the solid Rock,
> The Rock that shall forever more endure.
>> So let the storm clouds rise,
> The storm winds blow,
>> Let the rain come and go.
> For in Jesus, I am safe forever more.

> - Lanny Wolfe

The words of another great song state:

> Till the breaking of the dawn,
>> Till all footsteps cease to roam,
> Ever let this truth be known,
>> He remains the Cornerstone.

— ✧ —

Sermon 22

THE LAND AFAR OFF
Isaiah 33:17-24, 35:1-10

Introduction:

Ted Turner, media mogul, was honored as "Humanist of the Year." In his acceptance speech, this man, who had the audacity to rewrite the ten commandments, attacked Christianity. He said, "The more I strayed from my Christian upbringing the better I felt." In the speech, he said a very revealing thing. His sister died, after a lengthy illness, in spite of his prayers. He said of that experience, "If God is love and all-powerful, why does He allow these things to happen." Ted Turner had no eternal perspective. The Scripture says, "Hope deferred makes the heart sick." Turner saw death as a period, not a comma. He saw the future as a wall with no door. If there is no future life in a better world, Turner is right! Paul said, "If in this life only we have hope, we are of all men the most pitiable" (I Cor. 15:19). Turner had no hope beyond the graveyard!

Perhaps the greatest threat to faith is when life, whether by tragedy or by affluence, becomes focused on this world. If we have everything we want here, then we can be led to despair. If tragedy strikes, then life seems unfair.

There is a universal longing for a better world. Even the non-believer expresses it in efforts to improve this present world. Our hope is in a land we have not yet seen.

Isaiah lived in a time of epic struggle. He was affluent, being the first cousin to royalty, but the Scripture displays his longing for sights he had never seen in a "land afar off." The Scripture tells us that we shall see that land one day.

> There is a land that is fairer than day,
> And by faith we can see it afar,
> For the Father waits over the way,
> To prepare us a dwelling place there.

Isaiah reveals three sights we shall behold in that day:

I. **The Beauty of the King**

The Hebrew for *beauty* has several shades of meaning. It expresses natural beauty—a work of art, of action, of wisdom, of external and internal beauty. It also means splendid brightness and gracefulness. It was the word used to describe the regal beauty of Vashti in Esther 1:11.

The wonderful promise is that one day our eyes will behold the splendor of the Lord Jesus. It was this that our Lord prayed for on the night before His death, "Father, I desire that they also whom You gave Me may be with Me where I am that they may behold My glory" (John 17:24).

Years ago in Madagascar, those who were prisoners were required to work outside the prison. If the king or queen was scheduled to appear, they had to be back in the prison by noon. There was a law that stated that, if they saw the queen, they had to be set free so that they could salute her. Imagine a criminal slipping away and hiding until the sovereign appeared and then emerging. The law said that the chains were to be struck off and the prisoner was to say, "Is it well with you, my Sovereign?" Having gazed upon the beauty of the queen, he was forever set free.

That illustrates our privilege to look upon the Lord Jesus Christ, our "altogether lovely" King. However, we must see His blood before we see His beauty! Behold, His marred visage, His wounds, His bloody sweat, and His pierced body. Trust the dying Savior who bore our sins in His own body. One day we shall see Him as did the disciples of the Transfiguration, in blinding glory. We shall see Him as did John on Patmos, dazzled by His beauty.

> Fairest Lord Jesus, Ruler of all nations
> Thou of God and Man the Son.
> Thee will I cherish, Thee will I honor,
> Thou, my soul's glory, joy and crown.
>
> Beautiful Savior, Lord of all nations
> Son of God and Son of man.
> Glory and honor, praise, adoration
> Now and forevermore be thine.
>
> - anonymous

No mortal can with Him compare
Among the son's of men;
Fairer is He than all the fair
Who fill the heavenly train.

- Samuel Stennet

II. **The City of the King** (vs. 20)

Not only are we promised the beauty of the King, "Your eyes will see Jerusalem" (vs. 20). This wonderful prophecy predicts that day when the new Jerusalem will come down like a giant space station and hover over old Jerusalem! Abraham was looking for this city! Isaiah saw a day when Jerusalem would be the city of God. Back in Isaiah 1:21-23, he rebuked the wickedness of Jerusalem and all human cities. Then he promised that God's city would one day come (Isaiah 1:24-2:4). Hebrews 12:22-24 speaks of that heavenly Jerusalem, a city of angels, the church of the firstborn, the Old Testament believers, and Jesus!

John saw the city (Revelation 21:2-27). Such a sight fell upon his eyes. God's city—where we breathe in a deathless atmosphere, where tears will be no more, where death is vanquished, and heartache healed. Isaiah saw this city as a peaceful city (33:20), a permanent city (33:20), a healthy city, and a holy city (33:24). Think of it, no sin, no sickness, no war, and no moving. We live in a world where the average family will be moved five times. We are a generation that is rootless. In that day, the ships will no longer sail. No more moving—We will be home!

Just think of stepping on shore,
    And finding it heaven,
Of taking hold of a hand,
    And finding it God's,
Of breathing new air,
    And finding it heavenly air,
Of feeling invigorated,
    And finding it immortality
Of passing from storm and tempest to
    an unbroken calm,
Of waking up, and finding it Home!

III. **The Glory of the King** (35:1-7)

In that day, all nature will reflect the glory of the Lord Jesus. All nature that has been in discord since Adam's sin will be redeemed. Ecological balance will come. Man the polluter will no longer hold sway; the wilderness will flourish; the desert will blossom; rivers will flow clean and clear; life will spring with a glory not seen since creation. Our eyes will see this wonder!

Our eyes will see Jesus Christ coming. The eschatological glory will be ours to behold. God is coming to rescue us (35:3-4).

> The skies shall unfold,
>> Preparing His entrance.
> The stars shall applaud Him,
>> With thunders of praise.
> The sweet light in His eyes,
>> Shall enhance those awaiting.
> And we shall behold Him, then face to face.
>
> - Dottie Rambo

Also, we shall see the results of His work (35:5-7). In that day, the blind will behold, the lame will leap, the dumb will declare, and the deaf will hear! What a sight to behold.

Fanny Crosby, a dear blind saint, wrote many hymns. My favorite goes like this:

> When my life's work is ended
>> And I cross the swelling tide,
> And the bright and glorious morning I shall see.
>> I shall know my Redeemer
> When I reach the other side,
>> And His smile shall be the first to welcome me.
>
> I shall know Him, I shall know Him,
>> And redeemed by His side I shall stand;
> I shall know Him, I shall know Him,
>> By the prints of the nails in His hands.

Think of the countless miracle stories in the day of resurrection!

Conclusion:

Isaiah 35:8-10 describes the way to "the land far off?"

1. It is the *only* way. There is a highway to get us there (vs. 8). Jesus said, "I am the way." There is no other way but Him.

2. It is a *narrow* way. It is called a "Highway of Holiness" (vs. 8). No one in sin can get on that way without being forgiven and cleansed by Christ (See Matthew 7:13-14).

3. It is an *open* way (vs. 8). Notice it says, "whoever." The way to that land is open to all (See John 3:16).

4. It is a *simple* way (vs. 8). Even a fool, says our text, shall not go astray. Anyone can understand the simple gospel of Christ.

5. It is a *safe* way (vs. 9). Once a person sets foot on that way, neither Satan, lion nor beast can stop the journey to that land.

6. It is a *free* way (vs. 9-10). Only those who have been redeemed and ransomed may walk there. Our way has been paid in full by the sacrifice of Christ!

7. It is a *joyful* way (vs. 10). On that way, the people sing with everlasting joy.

Do you long for home? Remember the prodigal son? It was the thought of home that brought him to his senses. It was the knowledge of a better place that got him home.

> Oh land of rest, for Thee I sigh,
>   When will the moment come,
> When I shall lay my armor by,
>   And dwell in peace at home.

— ✧ —

Sermon 23

HOW TO LIVE IN VICTORY
Isaiah 36:1-37:38

Introduction:

For background, read Isaiah 36:1-5 and II Chronicles 32:7-8. The world is watching to see if the Glasnost and Perestroika of Gorbachev is real or just more Communist rhetoric. The little republics of Lithuania and Latvia are flexing the muscles of freedom. So far, the Russian response has been abusive and threatening. The *big bear* is growling at these smaller nations and their yearning for freedom.

This situation has its counterpart in Biblical history. Assyria dominated the world scene. Beginning in 1114 B.C. under Tiglath Pilesar I, the Empire spread from the Caspian Sea, westward across southern Russia to the Black Sea, south through Greece and Macedonia, across the Mediterranean to Egypt, Arabia, and Israel to the Persian Gulf. This Empire lasted for five hundred years. It would be Tiglath III who would begin troubling Israel. His successor, Shalmaneser V, would lay siege to Samaria in 725 B.C. His successor, Sargon II, would finally overrun Israel in 721 B.C. carrying the northern ten tribes captive to Assyria.

In 704, Sargon II would be succeeded by Sennacherib who would reign until 681 B.C. It is Sennacherib whom we encounter in our text. Having laid siege to Lachish, this tyrant issues a warning and then lays siege to Jerusalem. An inscription was discovered at Lachish, picturing the arrogant Sennacherib sitting on a throne, "Sennacherib, King of the World."

Sennacherib's vaunted boast against Jerusalem never came to pass. His own chronicles end with the siege. In three places, the Bible records the awesome victory of God! In one night, the angel of the Lord slew one hundred eighty-five thousand Assyrian soldiers. Sennacherib, nor Assyria, ever entered Judah again (II Kings 18-19, II Chronicles 32,

Isaiah 36-37). What a tremendous triumph! Tucked away in this narrative are abiding principles for living in victory.

I. **Know Your Foe** (36:1-20)

Bear Bryant once said, "Before you can learn how to win you must learn how not to lose!" A certain prescription for defeat is to be unaware of your enemy and his methods. Sennacherib is a picture of Satan and his forces besieging God's people and His church! Second Chronicles 32 offers some added details to Isaiah's account. These details teach us three facts about Satan that we must be alert to:

1. His Approach (II Chronicles 32)
The attack came on Isaiah during a great revival. Second Chronicles 32:1 says, "After these deeds of faithfulness." It was at a time of great spiritual refreshing that the approach came. Satan attacks at such times.

The attack was based upon that which was rational and sensible (36:16-17). Satan's offer is always sensible and appealing. God's ways require more than the natural.

His approach was religious in nature (36:5, 10-15). Sennacherib claimed that the Lord had sent him. He spoke the language of the people. He clothed his evil approach in religious language.

2. His Armor
Second Chronicles 32:8 sets forth the battle lines. Satan comes with the "arm of flesh." We have the Lord God! This wicked king arrogantly boasts against the Lord. Satan will always boast, bully, and threaten. Remember Goliath as he approached the boy David. We must let God do the battling.

3. His Attack (36:4-20, 37:14, II Chronicles 32:9-17)
Satan's approach is always the same. Sennacherib did not make a frontal assault. He sent gossips first (II Chronicles 32:9-16) to attack the God anointed and appointed leader. Hezekiah was scathingly attacked as the one who would lead them to destruction (II Chronicles 32:11). Then he was attacked for tearing up their religious traditions (II Chronicles 32:12). The attack came in the language of Israel (II Chronicles 32:18). Hezekiah answered with a prayer! Then the enemy began to write letters of attack.

Satan never changes! In a church when revival is nigh, the enemy will attack the leadership, undermining loyalty, threatening disaster, and questioning ability.

A church that will not follow God-called leadership will face defeat. The individual who does not live under the authority of God's word will face defeat. Satan always *discourages* and *divides* before he *destroys!*

II. Know How to Fight!

God never intended for us to live in fear, cowering before Satan. Satan will lay siege to our souls, only if we let Him. How can the battle be won?

1. Preparation (II Chronicles 32:1-5)
Hezekiah prepared the city and got the weapons ready for battle. Surrender is never an option. You need to claim your spiritual weapons (Ephesians 6:10-13).

2. Authority
The people listened to their leader—not the gossipers.

3. Faith (II Chronicles 32:7-8)
The battle was God's! Sennacherib's army greatly outnumbered Israel, yet they did not outnumber the army of God. God dispatched one angel to destroy the army of Assyria! Learn to believe the victory that is already yours in Christ.

4. Unity
Not one Jew broke ranks and gave in to the enemy!

5. Prayer and the Word (37:1-7)
Hezekiah, Isaiah, Eliakim, and Shebna called a prayer meeting. The only answer they sent to Sennacherib was God's Word given in answer to prayer. What was that answer?

    a.   We are not afraid!
    b.   You have blasphemed God!
    c.   A warrior angel is coming after you.
    d.   You are going to your own place.
    e.   You are a dead man!

Conclusion:
You can live in victory! A church can live in victory.

Jesus has won the victory. Romans 8:35-37 states the fact of victory clearly. Let Satan bring his biggest bombs, his thundering cannons, and his arrogant armies—"we are more than conquerors through Him that loved us."

Jesus loves you and hates hell's forces. Victory belongs to those who have received Jesus' victory at the cross. You do not have to live in defeat.

The battle of Waterloo was decided when Napoleon sent his famous cavalry at what seemed to be their weakest lines. However, Napoleon had failed to note a low place in the road. When the soldiers charged, Wellington's finest marksmen—who were hiding in the low place—rose and fired, stopping the charge of Napoleon and thus guaranteeing his defeat. Remember, when the enemy charges, standing in the low place in the road, is the victorious Christ! His blood always thwarts the enemy.

— ✧ —

Sermon 24

WHAT IF YOU KNEW YOU WERE DYING?
Isaiah 38:1-5, 39:1-8

Introduction:

There is nothing more certain than the uncertainty of life. For most people, death is as an unwelcome intruder who comes without warning. The Bible is replete with warning about the uncertainty of life and the relentless approach of death.

The Scriptures say: "For we must needs die and are as water spilt on the ground" (II Samuel 14:14). "For I know that thou wilt bring me to death" (Job 30:23). "There is no man that hath power over the spirit to retain the spirit; neither hath he power in the day of death" (Ecclesiastes 8:8). "And as it is appointed unto men once to die, but - after this the judgment" (Hebrews 9:27).

We all have an appointment with death, but seldom does God send notice of that appointment in advance. There have been a few times in history when God has sent the death notice. One of the most startling is found in Daniel 5:25-30 when drunken Belshazzar was warned by the mysterious handwriting on the wall.

The other prominent warning is found in our text. Hezekiah had a terminal illness. Isaiah came to make a pastoral call. Instead of comforting words and a prayer for healing, the prophet delivered a word from God, "Set your house in order for you shall die and not live" (Isaiah 38:1). Hezekiah prayed and God added fifteen years to his life. Before you praise the Lord for this answered prayer, let me point out that the nation might have been better off if Hezekiah had simply said, "Thy word and will be done."

Sometimes the worse thing that can happen is for our short-sighted prayers to be answered. God extended this king's life and in the third year of the fifteen, he had a son named Manasseh. Subsequent history and Scripture report that he was the most evil king to ever reign in the nation.

His reign lasted fifty-five long years. This wicked king built altars to the gods of paganism, and burned his sons to death as an offering to the demon god Molech.

Look at II Kings 21:9-11, 16. God sentenced the nation to captivity because of Manasseh. Look at the account of the invasion of Judah by Nebuchadnezzar in II Kings 24:1-4. It is written that this judgment came "for the sins of Manasseh the son of Hezekiah."

Also, because his life was extended, Isaiah 39 records that Hezekiah ignorantly displayed the wealth of the nation to Merodach Baladan, the crown prince of Babylon. Later, Babylon would come and seize the wealth of the nation.

What then should be the Christian's response to death? What if you knew you had only a year to live? What would you do? Let me share what I would do:

I. **Live Ready to Meet God.**

I believe the approach of death would cause me to want to be sure I am saved. I would want all sin confessed up to date. I would want old accounts settled. I would want the time left to be spent in faithful service to my Lord.

I remember when my little brother and friend, Mike Mashburn, came home to God, married, and seemed to have a promising life. Then he was struck with ALS. He chose not to be attached to a machine to live. During his time, He enrolled in *Christian Witness Training* and spent twelve weeks sharing Christ. When he went to the hospital for the last time, he asked me, "Where is my certificate?" I got it for him. Mike lived ready to meet God. He lived out the moving words of William Cullen Bryant in *THANATOPSIS:*

> So live that when thy summons comes to join
> The innumerable caravan which moves
> To that mysterious realm where each shall take
> His chamber in the silent halls of death,
> Thou go not, like the quarry-slave at night,
> Scourged to his dungeon, but sustained and
> soothed;
> By an unfaltering trust, approach thy grave
> Like one who wraps the drapery of his couch
> About him and lies down to pleasant dreams.

Let us not allow the approach of death to defeat us, rather let us embrace the Christ who is alive forevermore.

II. Love Those Close to Me.

Isaiah told the king, "Set your house in order." I would want my mate there if she chose to survive me. I would want my girls to come around and let me tell them all the things that never get said. I would want to tell my boy how to become a man. I would want all my family to know that I love them, and that I love Jesus. I would want to leave them a heritage of faith.

III. Loosen My Grip on the World.

How like the rich fool in Luke 12 we are. Somehow, we believe that material things are lasting. All that we have, God has given us to enjoy (I Timothy 6:6-10, 14-19). We are to enjoy things, but we are also to enjoy giving. You can only enjoy what you are willing to give.

IV. Limit My Time to Most Important Matters.

My priorities would change to those that really matter. Things that once seemed important would not matter anymore. All that I hoped to do one day would now be upon me. I would want to tell people about Jesus, and finish my course well.

Conclusion:

My favorite poet is Tennyson. On many occasions, I have read his reflections on death. When his best friend, Arthur Hallam, died, it was Christ who sustained the great poet as he wrote *IN MEMORIAM:*

> Strong Son of God, Immortal Love,
>   Whom we, who have not seen Thy face,
> By faith and faith alone embrace,
>   Believers where we cannot prove.

When the time for my departure comes, may I not embrace death, but my Savior. Hear Tennyson again in *CROSSING THE BAR:*

Sunset and evening star,
    And one clear call for me!
And may there be no moaning at the bar,
    When I put out to sea.

Twilight and evening bell,
    And after that the dark!
And may there be no sadness of farewell,
    When I embark.

For though from out our bourne of Time and Place,
    The flood may bear me far,
I hope to see my Pilot face to face
    When I have crossed the bar.

Are you ready to die? One has well said, "You are not ready to live until you are ready to die!"

— ✧ —

Sermon 25

A FULL SHOWCASE-AN EMPTY WAREHOUSE
Isaiah 39:1-8

Introduction:

Hezekiah experienced the healing power of God, and fifteen years were added to his life. Shortly thereafter, the crown prince of Babylon sent letters and gifts to Hezekiah. He was so pleased that he gave the messengers the grand tour of the nation. The messengers saw the treasury, the armory, and the resources of Israel.

Isaiah challenges the pride and presumption of Hezekiah with the warning that these very messengers would one day come to pillage the wealth of the nation. In the 1950's, Dr. Herschel Hobbs preached a sermon on this text and I have borrowed his title, "A Full Showcase But an Empty Warehouse."

Hezekiah's kingdom was prosperous and peaceful. The nation enjoyed the benefits of God-blessed prosperity. The warning of Isaiah was not a blast against the blessings of prosperity, but a warning against the carnal corruption that could bring judgment on a nation. Consider a brief three-fold application of the passage. Any one or all of the following can have *A Full Showcase and an Empty Warehouse:*

I. Our Nation

1. America has tremendous resources.
All of the crises predicted by the *doom sayers* of the 1980's have proven false. The gas lines and warning of the Carter years gave way to one of the longest booms in American history.

Nay sayers today warn of the trade deficits and of foreign interests buying up America. Not so! If the income of Coca Cola was added to the trade figures, the imbalance would vanish. America is successfully shifting from an

129

industrial to an *informational* society.

The oil crises was a hoax. Today we have more resources than when the *one-worlders* were warning us of a shortage.

People talk about the good old days. I believe God has given us the most blessed and prosperous days we have ever seen. With less than 10% of the world's population, America has: 40% of the wealth, 35% of the manufactured goods, 34% of the autos, 50% of the trucks, 50% of the telephones, television, steel, electricity, radios, and appliances.

Look at the houses in which we live. The most modest house or apartment has indoor plumbing, electricity, and a refrigerator—luxuries one half of the world does not enjoy.

The great capitalist system has many more of the blessings of prosperity than other systems. God has blessed our nation. However,

2. America may have an empty warehouse.

It is not wealth nor weapons that determine the strength of a people. It is, rather, a nation's moral center, its ethics that will decide its fate.

The Judeo-Christian ethic has been discarded by this nation for three primary reasons.

a. Liberal politicians have been elected to public office and have been more committed to a humanistic one-world agenda than to the morals of our nation.

Our Congress, after a year of debate, decided that haters of America can burn the flag without impunity.

Our courts fined Randall Terry $400,000 for a sit-in on the steps of an *abortuary* while fining AIDS-carrying homosexuals $100 for disrupting the services of Cardinal O'Conner of New York, by throwing AIDS infected blood on the worshipers.

We still have no amendment for voluntary prayer in school, though it is legal now for kids to have Bible clubs during free time at school.

The murder of the unborn continues in our nation. Pornography is moving unchecked into every area of society.

Drug and alcohol addiction are claiming more people every day. The occult continues to be sanctioned and approved under a New Age vocabulary.

b. Entertainment Industry
The major networks and most of the entertainment media are committed (80%) to the following agenda:
-One world government,
-Homosexuality as a normal lifestyle,
-Sexual promiscuity,
-Hatred of patriotism,
-New Age themes, (such as - God is merely a force with a light side and a dark side),
-Pro-abortion,
-Paganism and,
-Anti-Christian bias.
Presently, homosexuality is widely promoted on television. Movies like *THE LAST TEMPTATION OF CHRIST* have been bombs while movies like *CHARIOTS OF FIRE* and *DRIVING MISS DAISY* have been successful. Why does Hollywood continue to make blasphemous films? Money? Yes, but also the liberal community has an agenda.

II. A Church

With mainline denominations ordaining homosexuals to ministry, denying the inerrancy of scripture, embracing new age lingo and technique, substituting humanism for missions, and ignoring the hungry hearts of their people for God's word, America will continue to decline.

Some of you hearing this message are in a church where once Christ and the Bible, heaven and hell, sin and salvation, and spiritual strength were preached. Now you have messages on self-esteem, the feminist agenda, pro-abortion, and humanism. Friend, if you can't change it, don't support it. Find you a conservative Bible-teaching church!

Recently, an Associated Press article quoted Richard Peck, of the United Methodists, as saying, "Your church is impoverished if only people who agree that Scripture is without error are allowed positions of leadership." It hardly behooves a liberal leader to make such a statement. The decline of Methodism can be traced to its loss of theological soundness and evangelism fervor.

George Younge, an executive of the declining American

and Northern Baptist Convention said, "Southern Baptists sat out the civil rights movement." If that is true, why is the Southern Baptist Convention the most ethnically diverse denomination in America? There are more than five hundred new ethnic groups starting churches each year?

Frankly, I believe that people are tired of dead denominationalism. The facts are clear. Bible believing churches of every denomination and of no denomination are growing.

Churches can have buildings, programs, reputation, and resources and still be dead. Revelation 3:14-19 describes such a church—A full showcase of religion but an empty warehouse of spiritual power (See II Timothy 3:5, 4:1-4).

III. **An Individual**

Outwardly, you may have it all together! Life is going well—but only when a reversal comes do you open the warehouse of your soul and see what is there. Life is more than the outward trappings of success and happiness.

Do you have heart resources that come from knowing Jesus Christ as Savior? Does the Lord inhabit your life? When the chips are down, can you turn to the Lord? When the bottom falls out of life, do the everlasting arms of God support you? Oh, dear friend, it is possible to have an outward religion, but an absence of God!

Conclusion:

God says to the *nation*, "Blessed is the nation whose God is the Lord;" to the *church*, "Preach Christ crucified and risen;" to the *individual*, "Without Me you can do nothing."

Ezra Taft Dawson said, "The Lord works from the inside out. The world works from the outside in. The world would take people out of the slums. Christ takes the slums out of people, and then they take themselves out of the slums. The world would mold men by changing their environment. Christ changes men, who in turn change their environment. The world would shape human behavior, but Christ can change human nature." Beloved, it is what is inside and unseen that really matters.

— ✧ —

Sermon 26

THE PATHWAY TO POWER
Isaiah 40:25-31

Introduction:

There is a strange new malady that has been discovered in these days. It is a chronic physical fatigue caused by a virus named Epstein-Barr Syndrome. Persons afflicted with this disease find themselves physically exhausted day after day. The nature of this awful affliction is still being explored.

As tragic as that illness may be, there is a far worse malady than this, and that is spiritual exhaustion. Spiritual exhaustion can be tied to physical exhaustion. What is spiritual exhaustion? You are spiritually exhausted: When church is a chore; when sin seems more attractive; when you lose the big vision and focus on minor matters; when you need human praise in order to be faithful; when your work is faithful but you are not fruitful; when you make decisions based on unhappiness or difficulties rather than the will of God; when you hide from problems; when you are upset with others who are enjoying the Lord; when you think the work is your responsibility alone.

These are some of the symptoms of spiritual fatigue. Now notice how you can know the strength of the Lord:

I. Realize the Enemies of Spiritual Power.

1. Spiritual fatigue is a sign of a sick faith (40:25-26). The power of God our creator is at our disposal. How can we not believe that He has forsaken us. The persons who are worn out spiritually have taken their eyes off God and are operating in the energy of the flesh.
2. Spiritual fatigue leads to self-pity (40:27). When we are spiritually exhausted, we believe God has let us down. Soon we are drowning in the juices of self-pity.
3. Spiritual fatigue is a sign that one has lost touch with God (40:28-29).

The cry is clear. God never gets tired. He never faints! Why? Because God takes His Sabbath! God hallowed one day in seven for rest and renewal. Strength is a gift from God!

4. Spiritual fatigue opens the door to the enemy (40:30). The young men here are soldiers weakened from the battle or lying mortally wounded in the bloody dirt of the battlefield. Stephen Olford says that the dissipation of sin and the duties of service draw spiritual strength. "Remember what Amalek did unto thee by the way ... how he ... smote ... all that were feeble behind thee, when thou wast faint and weary."

II. Realize the Essentials of Spiritual Power (40:31)

1. The essential of "waiting"
The word wait does not mean idleness. The word literally means *an expectant dependence*. It is an Old Testament synonym for faith. It speaks of a faith that waits patiently for the word of the Lord.

Suppose you are a member of the President's Cabinet and important decisions are handed to you to implement. You are simply waiting for the word and timing. What do you do? You certainly are not idle. You are faithful to the other responsibilities for which clear orders have been given and resources have been provided. You simply await the word of your leader.

Our waiting is not idleness but obedience to God's word. How often we have failed in our refusal to wait. Abraham failed to wait on God and raised up Ishmael through adultery with his wife's maid. God puts us in the waiting room so that He can prepare all things for His purpose.

   a. Waiting is God's schoolhouse for your spiritual growth (Psalm 25:5).
   b. Waiting nurtures our hope (Psalm 62:5).
   c. Waiting teaches us patience (Proverbs 20:22).
   d. Waiting renews spiritual strength (Is. 40:31).

2. The essential of "renewing"
The word "renew" literally means *to exchange a new thing for an old*. It is the same word found in Isaiah 9:10 for

changing sycamores for cedar trees, thus renewing the forest.

The process of renewing begins with the removal of the old that weakened you. You are to receive a new strength from God and thus be renewed. The strength you receive is His strength. Our "waiting" is not just "waiting on the Lord" but "waiting before the Lord." By praise and prayer we look to God who "neither faints nor is weary" and "gives power to the weak" (Isaiah 40:28, 29).

Waiting is worshiping God. Waiting is obedience to God. Waiting is loving God. Waiting is trusting and believing God.

III. Realize the Evidence of Spiritual Power (40:31)

What evidence can be seen in the life of renewed spiritual power?

1. Strong believers assume their spiritual position. The eagle flies when the air is purer, vision keener, and sounds quieter. There above the clouds new vistas unfold that can never be seen in the valley. "Life with wings" is the heritage of every believer. God wants us to soar into the "heavenlies" with our Lord and explore spiritual vistas hitherto unseen and unexplored. Perhaps this is what Paul meant when he speaks of "sitting in the heavenlies." There the believer worships and is engaged in warfare. The eagle is a magnificent warrior bird. Scientists tell us that the eagle can fly directly into the sun because of a special lid that protects the retina. The renewed and empowered life is equipped to soar into the light of our Lord's presence?

2. Strong believers pursue their spiritual obligations. Running pictures our duties as soul-winners. Hebrews 12:1-2 speaks of life as a race. There are some things that demand the strength of a runner.

Those who are marathon runners must train and practice until the race. The undisciplined will never run the race.

In Acts 8:29, notice that Philip "runs" to the chariot to share the gospel with one Ethiopian.

3. Strong believers display spiritual dedication.
The word "walk" speaks of the "daily grind." The normal vocations of life or the routine can be a killer. The strengthened believer will stay by the normal commitments of life.

For instance, the strengthened believer will be as fired up about a regular service as a revival service. A strengthened believer will enjoy singing in the Sunday choir as much as a special program or solo part. A strengthened believer will not quit but will "walk" on with God through the normal grind.

Conclusion:

You can be strengthened today for the experience of life. Are you willing to wait? Are you willing for God to chop down the "sycamores" you planted and "renew" the forest of your life with His "cedars?" Will you get down before God and admit you are without strength and power?

One night on the stream Jabbok, Jacob met God. God wanted to deal with Jacob but Jacob was in a hurry. They got into a fight—a wrestling match! Jacob wanted to leave, so God knocked his hip out of joint. Then Jacob waited and, by sunrise, the blessing came. The word to Jacob was, "You are Israel, for as a prince you have power with God and men and have prevailed." If we will wait and not wrestle, God will give the power.

— ✧ —

Sermon 27

FACING YOUR FEARS
Isaiah 40:9-10; 41:10-14; 43:1-7; 44:2-3

Introduction:

Throughout this section of Isaiah, the phrase "fear not" appears repeatedly. Fear is a most debilitating emotion. Though we are called to "fear God," that particular word means to reverence, respect, or hold in awe. The fear found in these passages is the kind that damages personality, cripples ambition, and paralyzes action.

Across the panorama of these verses, there are four repeated themes that should put to rest the fears of every child of God.

1. The Greatness of God (Isaiah 40:12-28, 41:2-4, 42:5-8, 43:10-13, 44:6-8)

These are a few of the references on the greatness of almighty God! His greatness is visible in creation. It is evident in the nations. No one can view the magnificence of the universe and deny the greatness of God.

2. The Grace of God

Repeatedly, God speaks to His people as both Jacob and Israel. The name Jacob represents the flesh, the unredeemed nature of God's people. Israel was the race God gave a transformed Jacob! In Isaiah 41:8; 43:1, 22; 44:1-2, 21, God speaks of His sovereign choice of the people. In fact, Isaiah 41:14 refers to Jacob as a "worm" until God's power makes him a prince. Isaiah 43:25 speaks of the forgiving grace of God.

3. The Government of God

The fact that God governs in the affairs of this life is clearly declared in these verses. He is Lord. Though humanity is like "grass" and "the grass withers, "the word of our God stands forever" (Isaiah 40:8). He is Lord of Nature (40:12-14). He is Lord of the nations (40:15,23).

4. The Gospel of God

These chapters declare "good tidings" (40:9-11). The "good news" is that the Lord is coming to shepherd His people. Now look at Isaiah 40:9, "be not afraid." The coming of Jesus Christ is the end of fear! When He was born, the angels said "fear not." When John met Him at church on the Isle of Patmos, Jesus said, "fear not." When He comes, there is the death of fear. Notice in these chapters the defeat of our worst fear.

I. **The Fear of Loneliness** (Isaiah 41:10)

One of the greatest fears is the fear of being alone. The infant cries at the absence of its mother. The grieving widow feels the intense loneliness of life. It is reported that the aging actress, Rita Hayworth, set off the fire alarm regularly just to have someone to talk to.

The loss of a mate, a boy or girl friend, or a close companion can be a devastating blow. It can come by death, divorce, break-up, or simply a transfer. Others find themselves alone as the years pass by. Is there an answer?

Look at Isaiah 41:8-10 and rejoice! God is our friend. He says, "Fear not, I am with you." Certainly we need human friends. Yet, in the loneliest moments, Jesus is there.

When I was in seminary, several of us young preachers ministered at the rescue mission operated by the Home Mission Board. More than one hundred men were housed and fed. Derelicts and street people filled that place. Often, we would ask which song they wanted to sing. Every time, they wanted to sing, "What A Friend We Have In Jesus." I believe because there was an eternal loneliness in the depths of their sin-scarred souls. You need Jesus as a friend if you fear loneliness.

Max Lucado tells of visiting an old cemetery and reading the epitaphs. He came upon one on the grave of Grace Llewellen Smith. It said, "Loved, but loved not, Tried to please, but pleased not, Died as she lived, alone! God never intended for anyone to live that way. Jesus Christ was what this poor woman needed.

II. **The Fear of Sinfulness** (Isaiah 41:14)

One of the great barriers to wholeness of life is guilt. I'm not talking about guilt feelings, but genuine guilt. When one sins, that person is guilty before God. Unless that person comes to God, he stand at the bar of his own conscience. If his conscience is hardened, and that can happen, ultimately, that person will face judgment before God.

Our society wants to blame everything on social conditions, background, or circumstances. People do not steal because they are poor, but because they are sinners. What a person needs is not an excuse for sin, but a pardon for sin. Even though in our wickedness we are worms, God has redeemed us and brought us back. Jesus paid for our sins on the cross.

III. **The Fear of Unfairness** (Isaiah 43:1-4)

The passage before us needs to be understood clearly. You and I will pass through deep waters. We shall walk through the fiery flames of adversity! When that happens, we are tempted to cry "unfair." Young people can be heard saying it repeatedly, "That's not fair." No, the world will never seem fair. There are inequities that will be with us until Jesus comes.

Why does God allow such unfairness? So that we will learn that He is with us, and that which really matters cannot be "sunken in the sea" nor "drowned" nor burned up. Yes, you may feel pain in your flesh. You will know heartache and hurt, but the things that really matter will never be destroyed. God will balance the books in the next world.

IV. **The Fear of Meaninglessness** (Isaiah 43:5-7)

Many are afraid that their life has no great meaning or purpose. In Solzhenitsyn's work, *ONE DAY IN THE LIFE OF IVAN DENISOVICH*, we see that fear. A normal Russian man plods through a world where he is a nameless number without position or privilege.

Do not be afraid of insignificance. These verses tell us that God knows where his children are. The Jews were afraid they had been forgotten in exile. Yet God knew where they were. Isaiah 43:7 says of all God's children, "Whom I have created for my glory." We are here for the glory of God. The moment you come to Jesus you become eternally significant. You can then make an eternal difference in the lives of others. Kirkegaerd wrote one hundred thirty years ago, "If, when death comes, life is well spent, that is, spent so that it is rightly related to eternity—then God be praised eternally. If not, then it is irremedial—One only lives once."

V. **The Fear of Emptiness** (44:2-3)

There are those who immerse themselves in activity because the moment they pause, they feel an inner emptiness. There is a thirst for real life in every soul. There is a hole in every heart that only the living Christ can fill.

Our text promises fullness of life to all who will believe. God tells us not to be afraid of the emptiness of life, "I will pour water on Him that is thirsty."

As a Christian, I do not want my life to be a sham, an empty ritual of attendance and form—I want to know the fullness of Jesus Christ. I do not want to be empty.

The Answer To Fear:

1. Of loneliness - God's presence and people
2. Of sinfulness - God's pardon
3. Of unfairness - God promise
4. Of meaninglessness - God's purpose
5. Of emptiness - God's power

How do you get rid of fear? I John 4:18-19 tells us, "There is no fear in love; but perfect love casts out fear." Fear is a "spirit" that must be cast out. When we live in fear, Satan can torment us. God's love and love for God casts out fear! Loving Jesus and receiving His love releases you from fear. Loving others releases them from fear.

Our God is great, good and gracious. He has said, "Fear not." "Fear not" is another way of saying, "I love you."

— ✧ —

Sermon 28

THE THIRST FOR REVIVAL
Isaiah 43:18-44:5

Introduction:

A mother gave her little girl her birth certificate to carry to school for her records. She said, "Now honey, don't lose it." But the little girl did lose it and she was sitting on the steps of the school building weeping. Her teacher asked, "Why are you so upset?" The little first grader said, "I've lost my reason for being born." (Adrian Rogers)

This humorous story pictures a truth. Many of God's people and God's churches have lost their reason for being born again! They fill a pew, but are empty inside. They attend classes to fill their heads but their hearts remain empty. They fill their lives with activity for God, as if activity could make up for the awful absence of life.

Many saints have found themselves dry and barren in the Christian life. Churches have planted new converts in the dry fields of organized classes where there is no life. Soon, the new convert is dry and lifeless as well. Life communicates life! Peter Lord shared with me recently that "Christianity is more caught then taught!" Unless the leadership has the fresh flowing life of God, there will be no growth or discipleship. How we need the fresh, flowing fountains of God's life through our church! This passage displays *God's grace* and *man's responsibility* in revival. Please note three great truths regarding revival:

I. The Immutable Covenant of Revival (44:1-2)

Revival can happen because it is immutably promised by God. In His sovereign grace, He has promised revival to his people. Notice in 44:1 the little word "yet." This word points back to Isaiah 43:22-28. These verses list the tragic failures of God's people. Five disturbing attitudes characterized the people: *Prayerlessness* - 43:22a, *Weariness*

43:22b-23, *Stinginess* - 43:24a, *Sinfulness* - 43:24b, *Forgetfulness* - 43:25-28

Here are God's people who were going along carelessly serving God. God says to them. "You have wearied me and burdened me." They had forgotten God. Here are characteristics of hearts that need revival.

Notice again that word "yet." It pictures God's glorious covenant and promise to His people. "Yet," says God, "I have chosen you, I made you, I fashioned you, I have forgiven you, and I will help you." You see, revival is promised to us—not because of what we are or do but, because of God's love and grace toward us. We are like "Jacob" which means *to supplant or deceive.* But we are chosen to be "Israel" which means prince of God and "Jehuran" which means *justified one.*

God looks at our prayerlessness, sinfulness, and forgetfulness and says, "I will bless you with revival." How then can this revival come?

II. The Indispensable Condition for Revival (44:3)

In this verse God says, "I will pour water upon him that is thirsty." This promise has only one condition. The believer must be thirsty for revival.

I am convinced that the reason revival has not come in its fullness is because people are not thirsty enough. When a person is thirsty enough for water, he will do most anything for a drink. Spiritually, we are not thirsty enough. We are satisfied with the stagnant pools of a secular world. We are satisfied with the wells of the world. When was the last time you sensed Jesus living out His life through you? When was the last time you rejoiced in the forgiveness, righteousness and power of the Lord? Note these verses regarding thirst: *Prayer* - Psalm 42, *Praise* - Psalm 63, *Hearing the word* - Isaiah 55, *Righteous life* - Matthew 5:6, *To be a blessing* - John 7:37, *Overcome* - Revelation 21:6-7, *Desire to see Jesus* - Revelation 22:17-21.

David felt that thirst in Psalm 42:1-2, "As the deer pants after the water brooks so pants my soul after Thee, Oh God. My soul thirsts for God."

Again, David says in Psalm 63:1-2, "O God, Thou art my God, early will I seek Thee, my soul thirsts for Thee, my flesh longs for Thee in a dry and thirsty land where no water is, to see Thy power and Thy glory." Isaiah saw that thirst in Isaiah 55:1, "Ho! Everyone that thirsts, come to the waters." That is the condition of revival.

Jesus set forth this condition in two places. In the sermon on the Mount He said, "Blessed are they that do hunger and thirst after righteousness for they shall be filled" (Matthew 5:6). He is our righteousness, and when we thirst for Him, we shall not be disappointed. In John 7:37 Jesus said, "If any man thirst let Him come unto me and drink." We must be thirsty for God. As the salt of the earth, we ought to make each other thirsty for God.

In Revelation 21:6 Jesus says, "I will give of the fountain of the water of life freely to him who thirsts." Revelation 22:17 says, "let Him who thirsts come."

You see, as long as we are satisfied to hear about Jesus, sing about Jesus, talk about Jesus, and yet not have a living relationship with Him, there can be no revival.

The Lord wants us to seek His presence in our lives. We must want Jesus in our lives. You may say, "God knows I am empty." My car has been empty, but never thirsty! Is there a scorching thirst in your heart for the Lord? A thirsty person will pay any price for water—A spiritually thirsty person will pay any price for His presence.

Adrian Rogers said, "I don't know how much of God you have, but you have all you want." We have become satisfied with less than God wants us to have.

> Oh tell me Lord, that thou art mine;
> What can I wish beside?
> My soul shall at the fountain live,
> When all other streams are dried.

III. The Inevitable Consequence of Revival (43:3-5)

When God's people get thirsty, then God pours out blessings upon blessings. Revival blessings will come to the individual. God does not just give us a sip; He pours out His blessings in abundance.

Blessings come on the home as children receive the Spirit and blessings from God. Revival in this generation could mean a godly heritage for the next generation. Revival will cure the problems of youth. If a young person ever experiences the reality of the power of God, nothing less will ever do for him again.

Blessings will come on the church as growth occurs. Lost people will make professions of faith. They will "engrave God's name on their hands." This is a mark of ownership. Sinners will come to the Lord. Fruitful work happens as an overflow of revival.

> Revive us, Lord; zeal is abating,
> While harvest fields are vast and white;
> Revive us, Lord; the world is waiting;
> Equip Thy church to spread the light.

Are you thirsty for God, desiring His presence? Perhaps you're not saved and there's a deep thirst within for fulfillment. Today, you can come to the Fountain of Life and receive Jesus into your life. A sinful woman at Jacob's well heard Him say, "If you'll take the water I give, your thirst will be quenched." That sinful woman found Christ.

If you are saved, do you have a thirst for God in your life. Do you desire His presence. He said, "Ho! Everyone come." "If any thirst, let him come."

> Out of the hardness of heart and will,
> Out of the longings which nothing could fill,
> Out of the bitterness, madness, and strife,
> Out of myself and all I called life,
> Into the having of all things with Him,
> Into an ecstasy full to the brim,
> Jesus, I come, I come.

— ✧ —

Sermon 29

THE GOD WHO SAVES
Isaiah 45:18-25

Introduction:

We have seen the simplest things made complicated. My wife picked up a rewriting of a simple limerick.

"A triumvirate of murine rodents totally devoid of ophthalmic acuity were observed in a state of rapid locomotion in pursuit of an agriculturist uxorial adjunct. Said adjunct then performed a triple caudectomy, utilizing an acutely honed blade instrument generally used for subdivision of edible tissue." It is hard to believe that means the same as:

> Three blind mice, see how they run.
> They all ran after the farmer's wife
> She chopped off their tails with
> A carving knife.

Listen to this next one and see if you understand it! "A female of Homosapien species was the possessor of a small immature ruminant of the genus ovus, the outermost covering of which reflected all wave lengths of visible light with a luminosity equal to that of a mass of naturally occurring microscopically crystalline clear water. Regardless of the translational pathway chosen by the Homosapien female, there was a hundred percent probability that the aforementioned ruminant would select the same pathway." You wouldn't believe that means:

> Mary had a little lamb,
> Its fleece was white as snow,
> Everywhere that Mary went,
> The lamb was sure to go.

These complications are humorous, but in the matter of salvation, confusion and complication are dangerous and

145

deadly. Our text presents simply and clearly the way of salvation. There is life for a look. "Look unto me and be saved."

I. The Necessity of It (45:18-19)

Our text implies a universal need for salvation. Salvation means to be delivered from danger, rescued from ruin, and to be pardoned from peril. Man is lost and under the curse of the sin of his ancient father, Adam. The presence of evil and death is not an indictment against God, but against man who sinned.

God has spoken clearly to humanity in *creation*. He created the heavens. *Bara* is the Hebrew word for creation. It means to bring something out of nothing. From that matter, God "formed" the earth with a purpose. He made it to be alive, inhabited by people. Anyone should be able to see in the wonder of this planet and the glory of the universe the reality of God.

God has spoken in the *conscience* of man (vs. 19a). In verse 19, God says that He has spoken clearly to the heart of humanity — "seek Me." Seeking would not be in vain.

God has spoken in *Christ* (vs. 19b). God's righteousness was declared only in the person of Christ. Romans 1:16-17 says of the gospel of Christ, "For in it the righteousness of God is revealed from faith to faith." Jesus Christ is the only one who had ever lived totally right with God on this earth. Romans 3:21-22 declares, "But now the righteousness of God apart from the law is revealed being witnessed by the law and the prophets (including Isaiah), even the righteousness of God which is through faith in Jesus Christ to all and on all who believe." God has given us a way to be right with Himself through trusting Jesus Christ. God has spoken in the canon of Scripture "I declare things that are right" (vs. 19c). God's word can be trusted as right in every area where He speaks.

You need to be saved because you are lost in sin, because God made you for a purpose, and you are going to live forever in heaven or hell. "Look unto me and be saved."

II. The Exclusivity of It (45:20-21)

"Wait a minute," you might say, "I believe in a god and I have a religion. It really doesn't matter what you believe as long as you are sincere. Aren't we all going to heaven but by different roads? After all, I have my way and you have your way. Don't we all believe in the same God who has different names?"

Beloved friend, you may believe that, but you are fatally wrong! Look at Isaiah 45:14, 18, 21, 22. Notice the phrases, "no other," "no other God," "none besides Me." The first commandment indicated that there is only one God! The great God we serve is Elohim, the three in One, Yahweh, the God of the covenant, Jesus, the revelation of God as man (See John 14:6, Acts 4:12). There is no other God who can save (45:20).

None other Lamb, none other name,
    None other hope in Heaven, earth or sea,
None other hiding place from guilt and shame,
    None beside Thee!

III. The Simplicity of It (45:22-25)

How can a person be saved? First, there is the *word of truth* to be received. God has spoken (45:18, 19, 21). God has not only spoken, He has sworn by Himself (vs. 23). He has made an unchangeable oath and promise to save all who will come to Him by faith.

Second, there is the *look of trust* (vs. 27). This phrase reminds us of the serpent bitten people who were instructed to look upon a brazen serpent, lifted up on a pole, and live (Numbers 21:9). This incident was cited by our Lord to Nicodemus in John 3:14-16. In John 8:28, Jesus spoke of being "lifted up." In John 12:32, Jesus said, "And I, if I be lifted up from the earth will draw all men unto me."

We need to look unto Jesus! Look upon Jesus bowed in the agony of Gethsemane. Look at His shameful suffering on the cross. Behold the blood, wounds of dying love. See Him lifted up from the tomb to the very throne of Heaven. Look at Him with everlasting arms wide open to receive anyone who will come. Look away from yourself and your interests. Look away from any false hope.

Third, there is an *act of testimony* (45:23-25). We are to bow before our Lord and take an oath. We promise our allegiance upon our knees to the One who died for us!

Conclusion:

The greatest Baptist preacher, in my estimation, who ever preached was Charles Haddon Spurgeon. At age nineteen, he preached to the largest crowds in all of England.

Spurgeon's experience of salvation took place as he listened to a primitive Methodist preacher speak on this text. He had planned to go to another house of worship, but hindered by a blinding snowstorm, he slipped into the little Methodist chapel where only fifteen people were present.

Spurgeon said that for five years he had been in terrible distress and fear. "I thought the sun was blotted out of the sky and that I had so sinned against God that there was no hope for me."

Then Spurgeon heard the nearly illiterate preacher speak on this text. Said he, "My dear friends, this is a very simple text indeed. It says, "Look." Now that does not require a great deal of effort. It ain't lifting your foot or finger; it is just "look." Well a man need not go to college to look. You may be the biggest fool, and yet can look. A man need not be worth a thousand a year to look. Anyone can look. A child can look. Then it says, "look unto Me." Many look to themselves. No use looking there. You'll never find comfort in yourself. Look unto Me, I am sweating great drops of blood. "Look unto Me," I am hanging on a cross. "Look," I ascend. I am sitting at the Father's right hand. Oh, "look to Me."

Then the primitive Methodist spotted young Spurgeon and said, "Young man, you look so miserable. You will always be miserable —miserable in life and miserable in death unless you obey my text." Then the preacher shouted, "Young man, look to Jesus Christ now." Spurgeon said, "I did look to Jesus Christ. I looked until I could have looked my eyes away; and in Heaven I will look still in joy unutterable." (Criswell on Isaiah)

> I've a message from the Lord, hallelujah!
>   The message unto you I'll give!
> Tis recorded in His word, hallelujah!
>   It is only that you look and live!
>
> Look and live, my brother live!
>   Look to Jesus now and live!
> Tis recorded in His word, Hallelujah!
>   It is only that you look and live!
>
>   - unknown

It is in turning your eyes toward Jesus that you are saved. In that turning, you repent and are saved through faith in Him.

> Oh soul, are you weary and troubled,
>   No light in the darkness you see?
> There's light for a look at the Savior
>   And life more abundant and free.
>
> Turn your eyes upon Jesus.
>   Look full in His wonderful face,
> And the things of earth will grow strangely dim,
>   In the light of His glory and grace.

— ✧ —

Sermon 30

HOW STRONG IS YOUR GOD?
Isaiah 46:1-12

Introduction:

How strong is your God? Years ago, Dr. J.B. Phillips wrote a book entitled *YOUR GOD IS TOO SMALL*. In this book, Phillips pointed out that a person's faith was limited by his concept of God. He mentions such false images as resident policeman, parental hangover, grand old man, meek and mild, god-in-a-box, managing director, etc.

You could add to that list the impersonal force of the New Age ideology, a false god that is really self-worship. The ancient lie of Lucifer in Eden was "Ye shall be as gods." Now the New Ager's say, "We are gods."

The danger in those false concepts is that your view of God will affect your life for time and eternity. Isaiah's prophecy sets forth the worthiness of our God in contrast to the weakness of false gods.

I. **Our God Is Superior.** (46:1-2, 5-7)

Here is a ludicrous picture that would be humorous if it was not so tragic. The scene is of the nation of Israel going into captivity. Along with their household items, they are carrying their gods. "Bel" is the same as Baal who was the god of immorality. "Nebo" translates the Hebrew word for *oracle*. These two false gods speak of degradation and deceit.

These people prayed to these gods and yet they could not and did not answer them to deliver them from captivity. So often they go to be enslaved, still clinging to their false gods. The gods that they believed should bear them up, are a burden to them and their animals. These false gods have bowed to the judgments of the true God.

In verses 6-7, we discover that these false gods are bought and wrought in the image of man. These gods must be carried by the worshiper. They cannot move to help. They cannot hear your cries and prayers. They cannot save!

The God who has revealed and offered Himself to this world in Jesus Christ is vastly superior to the false gods of every age. Religion is a load—Christianity is a lift. Religion takes—Christ gives.

The saddest thing in the world is the lostness of religious people, some going into captivity to sin, to Satan, and to self, clinging to a worn out religion. Others, indulging themselves in fleshly sins, worship Bel, while others blindly follow Nebo, the false prophet of religion.

I look at our day and see people hopelessly burdened by a life without God, and others who look to religion and find no lasting help. It is not that God has not helped; it is that people do not know God. They have an idea or concept of God, but have not come to know Him personally.

II. Our God Is Strong. (46:3-4)

This is a wonderful picture of our Lord. He is the God who speaks clearly to us, the God who caries us through all the stages of life. He is with us from birthing to death rattle and beyond!

Notice God's self-portrait in His statements. In verse 3, God speaks of himself as watching over the birth of a child and, literally, "from the mother's lap." That speaks of tender care and concern.

> "I am He" - speaks of His presence
> "I will carry" - speaks of His power
> "I have made" - speaks of His purpose
> "I will bear" - speaks of His pardon

The word "bear" is not the same as "carry." It means to exalt, to lift, to elevate. It speaks of lifting a load up high. It is the same word used in Leviticus 22:9, and Numbers 18:32 for the priest in bearing sin and God in pardoning sin. It is used in Isaiah 53:4, 12 prophesying of Jesus bearing our griefs, sorrows and sins. Here the word "bear" is in the future tense speaking of the death of Christ which was still 700 years away for Isaiah.

In Isaiah 46:7, the same word "bear" speaks of the person who has a "god" of his own making. That "god" is a burden lifted up on the shoulders of the lost person.

Our God is not a burden to weight you down in disappointment and despair; He will carry you throughout life and into eternity. And He is a God who is strong enough to carry all of our burdens.

III. Our God Is Sovereign. (Isaiah 46:8-11)

As sovereign, God is exalted without peer in all realms. As sovereign, He does not simply know the end from the beginning, He declares and decrees the end from the beginning (46:10).

God is in control of history! He is Lord of the future. His Word shall stand. God will do exactly what pleases Him.

You and I are not on a collision course with fate, we are living under the authority of God! God's perfect will shall be done. We may not see it now. That is not important. It is important, rather, that we know, love, and trust Him!

IV. Our God Saves. (Isaiah 46:12-13)

Human beings are stubborn. We want our own way. This is the second time in these verses God has called upon the people to respond (vs. 3). He has called them also to remember. They are to remember who He is and what He has done.

These stubborn people are also sinful people. They are "far from righteousness" (vs. 12). Therefore, they need to repent.

God's desire is to save stubborn and sinful people! God has brought salvation near. God has brought salvation to us now. All who will respond to His word, repent of their sin, and remember His work for us will be saved.

Conclusion:

Recently, an Hispanic man was struck on a busy highway. Seriously injured, he crawled to the median of the interstate. He cried and waved for help, but nobody stopped. He laid injured for three days and nights. Finally, someone stopped at a phone and called the police. Miraculously the man survived.

How many are lying wounded by sin on the busy highways of life crying, out to gods who cannot hear, see nor save? Our Lord told the story of the good Samaritan. Finding the injured man, he cared for him and carried him on his donkey to an inn. Dear friend, that Samaritan is Jesus! He finds us, binds up our wounds, pays our way, and will one day return for us.

— ◇ —

NEW AGE OR OLD OCCULT
Isaiah 47:8-15, 57:3-18

Introduction:

These verses constitute a prophetic look at the fall of a mighty civilization and culture, Babylon. When one scans the panorama of history and views the collapse of world empires and nations, lurking behind the scenes is the occult. Babylon was no exception—Neither was Israel. Long before the military of Babylon came, the mysteries of Babylon came. Israel fell spiritually long before they collapsed militarily. Thus, Isaiah 47 chronicles the sad collapse of Babylon while Isaiah 57 records the nation Israel following the same course.

I. The Description of the New Age Movement

Strangely our day has seen the rise of a new interest in the spiritual, mystical and transcendent. In their new book, *MEGATRENDS 2000*, Naisbett and Aburdedene predict a spiritual awakening in this decade. This awakening, however, is not only of Christianity, but of the new age movement.

REVEALING COMMENTS BY NEW AGE CELEBRITIES:

1. "When business people come in and start opening up the process, there's nobody who changes faster, and I think there are several reasons for this. First of all, you're dealing with top level executives. These are people who have entrepreneurial minds, which means they are risk-takers. Also, various studies have shown that business executives tend to be right-brained, or at least quite spontaneous, creative and intuitive in their thinking. And they are also extremely pragmatic: they're interested in anything that works."
(Marilyn Ferguson, author of *AQUARIAN CONSPIRACY*, in an interview for *NEW AGE MAGAZINE*)

2.   "I am God!"
(Shirley MacLaine, in the 1987 TV mini series, *OUT ON A LIMB*)

3.   "I see yoga and crystals as tools to get me where I want to go: I want to go home. I want to go to the place where it's always safe to be myself—always and in all ways. I want to achieve permanent peace. That's what life is all about, isn't it?"
(LeVar Burton, star of *STARK TREK: THE NEXT GENERATION*)

4.   "All of us who postulate a loving God, and really think about it, eventually come to a single terrifying idea: God wants us to become Himself (or Herself or Itself). We are growing toward godhood. God is the goal of evolution. It is God who is the source of the evolutionary force and God who is the destination. This is what we mean when we say He is the Alpha, and the Omega, the beginning and the end. It is one thing to believe in a nice old God who will take good care of us from a lofty position of power which we ourselves could never begin to attain. It is quite another to believe in a God who has it in mind for us precisely that we should attain His position, His power, His wisdom, His identity."
(M. Scott Peck, *A ROAD LESS TRAVELLED*)

5.   "I am convinced that the battle for humankind's future must be waged and won in the public school classroom by teachers who correctly perceive their role as the proselytizers of a new faith: a religion of humanity that recognizes and respects the spark of what theologians call divinity in every human being."
(John Dunphy in his award-winning essay, *A RELIGION FOR A NEW AGE*)

This movement is a loosely organized network of religious, educational concepts, that are an ever-changing range of values, trends and beliefs (Russel Chandler). A summary of beliefs is hard to nail down because there are many divergent beliefs in the movement. What are their false or distorted views?

1.   Man is God! (47:8)
The new ager believes that he is god, a law unto himself.

Shirley MacLaine has said, "I am God."

The new age is an extension of Hinduism which allows one to believe almost anything. It is a cult that can accept from all religions. They believe that man has a spark of the divine in himself. That he simply needs to move to a higher consciousness in order to discover the god that is in him.

2. Nature is God.

All nature becomes god as well. Many new agers believe in reincarnation. Man may return after death as another person or an animal. That is why it is not incongruous for new agers to support abortion (this child will be back as a part of nature), while saving the whales (that may be a reincarnated person).

Listen to me very carefully. Most of you are being exposed to occultic, demonic, new age practices in school, job training, self-improvement courses, but most of all, entertainment.

In business, most of the Fortune 500 companies are requiring employees to attend such sessions. Occultists with Ph.D's talk about focusing on an image or imaging, channeling, chanting, meditating by which the individual gives over control to some inner force (i.e. the god inside you).

In entertainment, more and more strange movies with interaction with dead people are being made. *FIELD OF DREAMS*, while entertaining, has shoeless Joe Jackson coming back from the dead to play ball. *Karma* is the buzzword of the new age movement in that movie. In *STAR WARS*, every person has access to the force, an impersonal god-like power that has a dark side and a bright side. In that concept, God is also the devil! This lie is as old as Eden where Satan said to man, "You shall be as gods knowing good and evil."

3. One can do what he pleases (47:10).

The new ager does not believe in sin. He simply believes one is in harmony or out of sync with himself and nature (47:8). Pleasure seeking and moral wickedness are good as long as you stay in harmony. In other words, if it feels good, do it.

4. There are spiritual forces one can tap (47:12-13).

In our text, enchantments, sorceries, astrology, and astral projection are mentioned. Enchantments include crystal gazing, ornaments, and symbols. We are to call them "good luck charms."

Sorceries include the use of *channels* to assist in contacting the spiritual force. They are called *mediums* or *witches*. In truth, they become the instruments of demons.

Astrology is the belief that the location of the stars and planets affects one's life. People believe they live under a sign of the zodiac. One's horoscope is the prediction of the affects of the stars on one's date of birth.

Astral projection holds that you can, with the aid of the force of stars, leave your body and go to another place.

These things may seem foolish, but our children are being sold toys that are occult symbols, characters, and concepts. Our schools are permeated with this new wave of consciousness raising as an educational tool. Business people are being trained in new age philosophy. We are being bombarded by their philosophies.

II. The Danger of the New Age Movement

There is a network of groups, agencies, religions, and individuals that are committed to taking over the world. The method of take over is infiltration and indoctrination. Why is it dangerous?

1. Because its view of God and man is false.

God is separate from us and above us. Man is a created being who is responsible for his actions. He is capable of wrong. It is not that he is not in harmony with himself and nature, but that he is out of sync with God.

There is only one God who has revealed Himself in Christ. We cannot be Jesus Christ, but we can be saved by Him, be indwelt by Him, be loved by Him, be transformed by Him. In knowing Him, we become the highest possible self!

2. Its vision of civilization is dangerous.

One nation that is primarily Hindu in philosophy is India. While many wonderful things have come from that land, it has remained very poor. Its view of man allows a caste system whereby millions live in dire poverty. (Bad Karma -

Maybe they will come back as a higher cast later.) The upper classes believe that they deserve to be well off because of a past life that was better. Animal rights are preserved (millions of cows worshiped, rats eating the food) while people starve.

Hitler was an occultist belonging to a group called the Thule group. He believed it was possible to create a super race of individuals and that the inferior ought to die.

3. Its methods invite satanic invasion and control. When a person submits his mind to be controlled by some alien power, he has invited satanic control.

4. It has a warped view of reality (47:10).

Conclusion:

The interest in spiritual things in our nation is a signal that people are tired of atheism and scientism. People are looking within and beyond for something more. We must not simply stand around hurling criticism at the new age movement. Now is the time for those of us who know Christ to step into the void and say to a spiritually starved and seeking world:

1. Yes, there is a God who loves you, a personal God you can know who will reveal Himself to you.

2. Yes, your life can be transformed and be a higher life than you ever dreamed possible. It is not through your own works or efforts, but by admitting your sins and failures and turning to the historical Jesus who died for you and was raised bodily from the dead.

3. There is a life beyond the grave, but it is a life that honors who you are! You do not need to come back as another. There is a better world for redeemed and trans-formed human beings. We will not float around as spirits—we shall live raised from the dead in a new body.

4. Spiritual values are more important than the material. Our world can be improved by saved people.

5. A new world and new age is coming when the Lord Jesus Christ returns to reign!

— ✧ —

THE KEYS TO A LIFE OF PEACE
Isaiah 48:16-22, 57:19-21

Introduction:

The Hebrew word for "peace," *Shalom,* occurs two hundred fifty times in two hundred thirteen separate verses in the Old Testament. The word means *freedom from disturbance, soundness, health, completeness, order* and *prosperity.* Girdlestone, the great Hebrew scholar, says that the concept of peace "implied a bringing of some difficulty to a conclusion, finishing off a work, a clearing away by payment or labor." Peace in the Old Testament is never simply the absence of strife—It is the state of being right with God, having one's life in order with God. Israel was making the sad choice of serving something other than the Lord. Because of that, life was out of order. Isaiah 48:10-11 reveals the chastening hand of God. Affliction came upon a people whose lives were out of order with God.

Peace is not the absence of tension—It is the presence of God! In Judges 6, we discover that peace is a part of the name and the nature of God. When you review this story, you find Gideon a man who wanted peace, but who could not live in peace because of the Midianites. These enemies pillaged the land, stealing whatever they liked. Gideon had a coward's peace. Hiding from the enemy, he thrashed his grain at night. Then God showed up and told Gideon, "Go knock down your father's altar, kill your father's prize bull, build another altar, sacrifice the bull, chop down the idol, Ashtoreth, and declare war on Midian!"

Gideon obeyed and named the place Jehovah-Shalom for, at last, he understood that peace is getting things in order with God. God did not come to get rid of tension, but to introduce it. This was not the end of war—It was the beginning! There was no peace for Israel in compromise with Babylon. There was no peace for Gideon in hiding from Midian and no peace for Gideon as long as the altar of tradition, built by his father, stood!

Listen, dear friend, there can never be order in your life if your life is out of order with God! "Peace is the deep-rooted sense of order that comes in the midst of tension and stress and hostilities, when you know that you are ordering your life according to the orders of the God of order" (Stuart Briscoe).

How can you have the shalom of God? How can you know peace? There are three lanes on God's path to peace:

I. Understand the Life of God (48:12-13)

Who is the God that calls you to peace? He is the God who was there before the world was! He is the God who will be on the throne when this world is no more! He is the God who spoke and the creation sprung from the energy of His Divine voice! Our text says that when God speaks all of creation "stands" at attention (vs. 13).

Also, this creation stands together! God put the creation in order. To our knowledge, only earth and humanity have dared to step out of order ("Stand" means to *stand ready to obey*). If the Lord Jesus can govern the galaxies, and hold all of matter together by His word, don't you believe that He can order your life?

One day the Lord Jesus said to the wild winds and the stormy sea, "Peace be still," and they said, "Yes, Lord." He said to a fish, "Bring me a coin from the sea," and the fish said, "Yes Lord." All of creation moves at His Word. Only man is out of order. If you want peace, then understand the life of God. This great God is calling you to Himself.

II. Experience the Love of God (48:14-16)

Israel had been sentenced to exile in Babylon for forsaking God. Yet there remained the "call of God." God's appeal remains because He loves the people. This word "love" speaks of the tender mercies of God in covenant with His people.

Our Lord calls us and loves us even when we are in captivity! He promises to prosper our way. If your life is out of order, you must heed the call of God's loving heart.

In verse 16, note the truth of the trinity! Here is the voice of the pre-incarnate Christ. "The Lord God and His Spirit have sent me." The word "have" is singular in Hebrew. God the Father and God the Spirit "have" sent Jesus! Jesus is the One who calls. He is the One who demonstrates the love of God.

Colossians 1:19-22 demonstrates the fulfillment of this promise. Peace came when Jesus went to war for us and shed His blood to make peace. An outraged heaven said, "It is enough." Into this world of disorder, the God of order came to call to order all who would trust Him (See Isaiah 57:19).

III. Follow the Leadership of God (48:17-22)

The third lane on God's path of peace is obedience to God. The Lord will teach us and lead us. We can have instruction and direction in life. Peace is absent when we do not know what to do, or do not know what direction to follow.

During the days of slavery, a group of slaves mutinied on a ship, and killed the captain and crew. None of them had ever been on a ship. When the ship was found they were bowing to the compass. They had freedom but they lacked instruction and direction. Soon they were enslaved again.

Friend, you can find freedom in Christ, but without obedience to the instruction and direction of Jesus, you will be shipwrecked or enslaved again.

If sin comes, then peace will leave (48:22, 57:20-21). God's peace belongs to those who order their lives according to His word.

Conclusion:

What are the blessings of peace?

1. Your life will be in the flow of God's will - "peace like a river" (48:18).

2. Your life will be a force for righteousness - "righteousness like waves of the sea" (48:18).

3. Your life will have a future (48:19).

4. You will experience freedom (48:20). This freedom

from your enemies will cause you to sing for joy.

5. You will experience the fullness of the Spirit (48:21).

This verse declares that the same God who gave water out of the rock will send the gushing waters of His fullness (Exodus 17:1-7, I Corinthians 10:4).

Romans 5:1 says, "Therefore being justified by faith we have peace with God through our Lord Jesus Christ."

Peace can be yours if you will understand the life of God, the love of God, and the leadership of God. The same God who called Israel is the Christ who calls you today. His peace awaits your response. If you refuse, "There is no peace saith my God to the wicked" (48:22; 57:21).

— ✧ —

NEVER ASHAMED OF JESUS

Isaiah 49:1-23

Introduction:

So much has been said about the late Bear Bryant of Alabama one hardly knows where facts end and legend begins. One such story I heard took place during the early days of his coaching career. There was a team meeting going on. The boys were tired from the summer practice, perspiring from the heat of the sun. Suddenly, an old man walked into the room. He was clean, but had on the uniform of a southern dirt farmer—overalls. His face was coarsened and brown from the sun. His big hands told the story of hard labor. His eyes squinted around the room. Bear Bryant asked, "Sir, can I help you." All of a sudden a big boy stood up and walked over to the man and said, "Coach Bryant, this is my grandpa—he raised me and encouraged me to be all that I can be." He then hugged that old man unashamedly. Coach Bryant turned to the boys and said, "Boys, don't ever be ashamed of those who helped you get to where you are today." Then looking at the old man he said, "Sir, it is an honor to see you." The old man said, "Coach, I just wanted to be sure you were taking care of my boy."

I have sadly seen young people grow ashamed of their humble beginnings. Worse than that, I have seen people grow ashamed of Jesus—acting as if they did not know Him.

Isaiah 49 presents the coming servant of the Lord, Jesus Christ. Verse 23 says, "They shall not be ashamed who wait upon (serve) Thee." According to Webster's New Collegiate Dictionary the word "ashamed" means, 1. *feeling shame, guilt,* or *disgrace,* 2. *feeling inferior* or *unworthy,* 3. *restrained by anticipation of shame.*

Our text reveals some of the reasons we should never be ashamed of Jesus.

I. **The Way He Came** (49:1)

This verse speaks of the divine origin of our Savior. He became like us, born a human being, that we might be like Him. He had no earthly father that we might have a heavenly Father. He birthed from the womb of His mother that we might be given a new birth. He said yes to our human plight and became one of us to save us.

II. **The Words He Spoke** (49:2)

It was said of our Lord, "Never a man spake like this." Jesus' Word was an implement of war, a sword. It can cut like a scalpel to heal; it can sever the chains that bind humanity; it can send the enemy in retreat.

In fact, His life is called a spear. There was a day when our Lord was pulled from heaven's quiver and fired at the enemy. The spear that pierced His heart also brought down the king of darkness. He came to be against everything that is against us (Romans 8:1-21).

The words of another mean little until you know the person who spoke them. A young lady bought a book and found it so boring she quit reading it after the first chapter. Later she married the author—Then the book became one of the best she had ever read. The words of Lincoln mean more when we see him killed for his convictions. Knowing Fanny Crosby was blind makes her hymns more beautiful. Far greater than all of that is knowing who Jesus is and what He has done. This makes His words precious unto us.

III. **The Will He Obeyed** (4-6)

Our text says Jesus came with a threefold purpose. *First*, He came to glorify the Father. *Second*, He came to gather the Jews. *Third*, He came to go after the Gentiles.

Our mission is the same today. Everything we do must be done to His glory. We are to go after those like us and those unlike us as well. The mission has not changed, nor has the message. However, the methods must change to use every means in harmony with Scripture to reach people.

IV. The Work He Finished (7-12)

The Lord's servant, Jesus, was *despised* that we might be *prized* (vs. 7a). He who should have been *adored* was *abhorred*. He became the *covenant* that would be *cut* for our sins. He was given for the sacrifice of the covenant. Every person who comes to the Father must come on the basis of the blood of the covenant (vs. 8). He came in order that those who are captive might be freed (vs. 9). Everything that would enslave you has been broken by Christ. He came to set the prisoners free. You must understand that you are an inmate, a convict, a prisoner of this world system. You cannot escape the *stain of sin*, the *lure of the lewd*, the *failing of the flesh*, nor the inevitable *darkness of death*. Trusting Christ brings light to those dark places.

He came in order to feed us (vs. 10a). He will also lead us (vs. 10b). I am not ashamed of the work our Lord finished. He is still *freeing, feeding,* and *leading* all who will come to Him.

V. The Worship He Deserves (13-23)

He deserves our worship for who He is! I can also praise Him for what He has done. I am not ashamed to worship Him because I am in the family (vs. 13-15). We are His children and God has placed us in His eternal memory.

I praise Him because of the wounds of His love (vs. 16). When the nails went into His hands, it was for me. Those scars have my name upon them.

I am not ashamed to worship because I am on my way to a wedding (vs. 18-23). This scene pictures God the Father clothing Jesus for the marriage supper. His clothing is the redeemed, both Jew and gentile. His necklace that sparkles and shines are those who have come to Him.

The redeemed Jews who had known captivity and persecution will see this and be amazed at all the children God has brought up. I believe all the babies that have died will be in heaven.

I am waiting for the wedding! My King is coming! It will be a glorious celebration. I am not ashamed to say I love Him!

168 / Light for Days of Darkness

Conclusion:

Have you trusted Christ? Would you be ashamed to say you are coming to Him?

I remember the story of a teenage girl who was ashamed of the scarred face of her mother. One day her mother, noticing the shame, sat the immature teen down and told her the story of the scars. When she was younger she had been beautiful. One day while hanging out clothes she looked in the window to check on the girl who was a baby. A log had rolled off the fire near the baby's crib and the blanket around the child had begun to burn. The mother ran in, grabbed the blanket and smothered the flame against her body. The flame scarred the upper body of the mother permanently. The mother received those scars saving the life of the daughter. The daughter grabbed her mother and kissed her face and said, "Mother I am sorry, you are beautiful to me." Our Lord bears the scars of love for us. Let us never be ashamed.

> Jesus! and shall it ever be,
> A mortal man ashamed of Thee?
> Ashamed of Thee, whom angels praise,
> Whose glories shine through endless days?
>
> Ashamed of Jesus? Sooner far,
> Let evening blush to own a star.
> He sheds the beams of light divine,
> O'er this benighted soul of mine.
>
> Ashamed of Jesus? Just as soon,
> Let midnight be ashamed of noon.
> This midnight with my soul till He,
> Bright Morning Star, bids darkness flee.
>
> Ashamed of Jesus, that dear Friend,
> On whom my hopes of heaven depend?
> No; when I blush, be this my shame,
> That I no more revere His name.
>
> - unknown

— ✧ —

Sermon 34

THE PRICE ON YOUR HEAD
Isaiah 50:1-11

Introduction:

Several years ago I heard Tony Campolo preach his famous message, *WHO SWITCHED THE PRICE TAGS?* The message idea came from a true incident. Several pranksters went into a store and switched tags on expensive articles with those on less expensive articles. Leather coats were then priced at $1.98 while a pair of socks went for $300.00! That was a humorous prank, but in reality someone has switched the price tags in our society. The things that matter the most are no longer counted as valuable, while the highest value is placed upon that which is cheap and temporary.

When we look at our American society, we can see that there is a tremendous loss of values. Human life, culture and morals are cheapened. Recently, the tax funded National Endowment for the arts was exposed. There was a time when a *Rembrandt, Van Gogh* or *Monet* were considered art. Today, a mason jar with a urine covered crucifix is valued at thousands of dollars. A go-go dancer receives seventy-five thousand dollars for a striptease act she calls art! When I think of the arts, I think of Van Cliburn at the piano, the symphony, and the great museums and galleries.

Our nation has put a cheap price tag on our Judeo-Christian heritage. Israel did the same thing. In the opening verses of our text we see God divorced from the mother of Israel. We see these children of that divorce sold into the slavery of sin (50:1). The condition of Israel is described in three ways:

1.   Divorce is the first illustration.
The certificate of divorce was issued by a husband who placed it in the possession of the wife. On the inside, it

169

described the cause, on the outside the price of reconcilia-
tion. She could show it to her family in hope of a settle-
ment that would restore the marriage. She could show it to
another suitor in hope of a remarriage.

Divorce left the woman abandoned and alone. Now,
biblical ground for divorce in the Old Testament was
adultery. Therefore, the sin of Israel is described as "transgression." Transgression means to cross *a forbidden
boundary, to break the law, to trespass on the property of
another.* These people had proved unfaithful to God,
therefore they were separated from Him.

2. The second metaphor is that of debt.
The people had sold out too cheaply. They had switched the
price tags on life. They were hopelessly in debt for that
which was only temporary. One of the most disastrous
things that can happen to a family is to go deeply into
financial debt. Literally, debt is selling yourself into bondage for things. Israel had discounted their value and sold
out too cheaply.

There was a man in Texas who saw all his neighbors
get rich with oil, but his land did not yield any. His neighbors all sold out and moved to the city and to an affluent
lifestyle. For years he questioned God as he worked his
ranch and reared his family. Fifteen years later his
children had grown into fine Christian adults. His marriage
was strong and his love for Christ had deepened. All of his
neighbors had seen prosperity spoil their lives. All were
divorced. There had been a suicide. Alcohol and drug
problems among the kids were common. He said, "I thank
God they did not find oil on my land."

3. The third metaphor is disinterest.
In Isaiah 50:2 when God knocked at the door, no one
answered. When he called, no one responded. Here was a
people who had grown unfaithful, unthinking and unresponsive to God.

Some of you are in that kind of trouble today. You
have sold yourself for temporary pleasure. You have taken
a divorce from God in your life. God has knocked at the
door of your life through business reversals, family prob-

lems, personal problems, addiction, and failure. When He knocks, you will not answer. When the doorbell of your life rings, you are never at home. You are covered up with situations that you cannot untangle. The bill collector of life has now presented you with the tab, and you do not have the resources to pay. What can you do? Admit that you need Christ!

I. You Need the Hand of Christ (50:2)

The word "redeem" represented a legal action in Israel. One who had sold property because of debt could redeem or buy back the land. This right could be exercised by any member of the family. This principle is seen in the book of Ruth. Naomi and her family left Bethlehem and lived in Moab after selling their property because of debt. When Ruth and Naomi returned, Boaz redeemed the land of Naomi and the widow, Ruth! A redeemer had to be a kinsman who was able and willing to redeem.

Our Lord's hand was a human hand. It was an able hand. It was a willing hand.

When my Savior reached down for me,
    When He reached down His hand for me,
I was lost and undone without God or his Son,
    When He reached down His hand for me.

II. You Need the Voice of Christ (Isaiah 50:4-5)

Our dear Lord will know exactly what to say to you. Remember what he said to the woman at Jacob's well. His word was honest, yet hopeful. Look at the woman caught in adultery. His word to her was convicting, yet compassionate. Look at Nicodemus. Jesus' word to him was stern, yet redemptive. Think of the prodigal who worried about what he could possibly say to the one he had failed so miserably. He never had to make that speech.

Jesus knows what to say to those who are worn out with the world, tired of being sick and tired. He said, "Come unto me all ye who labor and are heavy laden and I will give you rest."

III. **You Need the Scars of Christ** (Isaiah 50:6-9)

When you come to Jesus, you discover that He gave His back to those who beat Him. His beard was torn from His face. He did not turn away from "the shame and the spitting." All the punishment you deserve for selling out so cheaply, Jesus endured for you.

To the world, you are a number, a laborer, a product, a producer, a performer, a checkbook, a commodity, or an object of pleasure. Who really cares who you are on the inside? Look at the scars on the back and face of Jesus. See the spittle run down His face. He did not have to suffer like that, but He valued you that much.

Our scarred Savior has faced down our adversary (50:8). He is ready to give you value and victory. His wounds declare our worth!

IV. **You Need the Name of Christ** (Isaiah 50:10-11)

Our message ends with a call to faith. There is a reverence to be demonstrated. He is the Lord, revere His name! Jesus' name is not a curse word, but a confession of faith and a cry for help.

There is a voice to be obeyed. He is calling now to all who will hear! There is a faith to be exercised. You can trust the name of Jesus!

The option to this choice is unspeakable and unthinkable. Hell, according to verse 11, is the fire kindled by your own sins! "You shall lie down in torment." Dear friend, death is not lying down in peace. It is not the end of your problems. Without Christ, it is torment.

In February 1941, Maximilian Kolbe was incarcerated at Auschwitz. He was a Franciscan priest. In the harshness of the slaughterhouse, he maintained the gentleness of Christ. He shared his food. He gave up his bunk. He prayed for his captors. He was soon given the nickname, "Saint of Auschwitz."

In July of that same year, there was an escape from the prison. It was the custom at Auschwitz to kill ten prisoners for every one who escaped. All the prisoners would be gathered into the courtyard and the commandant would randomly select ten names from the roll book. These victims would be immediately taken to a cell where they would receive no food or water until they died.

The commandant begins calling the names. At each selection another prisoner steps forward to fill the sinister quota. The tenth name he calls is Gajowniczek.

As the SS officers check the numbers of the condemned, one of them begins to sob. "My wife and my children," he weeps.

The officers turn as they hear movement among the prisoners. The guards raise their rifles. The dogs are tense, anticipating a command to attack. A prisoner has left his row and is pushing his way to the front.

It is Kolbe. No fear on his face. No hesitancy in his step. The capo shouts at him to stop or be shot. "I want to talk to the commander," he says calmly. For some reason the officer doesn't club or kill him. Kolbe stops a few paces from the commandant, removes his hat and looks the German officer in the eye.

"Herr Kommandant, I wish to make a request, please." That no one shot him is a miracle.

"I want to die in the place of this prisoner." He points at the sobbing Gajowniczek. The audacious request is presented without stammer.

"I have no wife and children. Besides, I am old and not good for anything. He's in better condition." Kolbe knew well the Nazi mentality.

"Who are you?" the officer asks. "A Catholic priest." The block is stunned. The commandant, unusually speechless. After a moment, he barks, "Request granted."

Prisoners were never allowed to speak. Gajowniczek says, "I could only thank him with my eyes. I was stunned and could hardly grasp what was going on. The immensity of it—I, the condemned, am to live and someone else, willingly and voluntarily, offers his life for me, a stranger. Is this some dream?"

Conclusion:

If you have undervalued your life; if you have allowed sin to buy you at a discount—Remember, God loves you and values your life. You need to see His hand reaching down for you. His tender voice is calling you. His scars declare His love for you. Let Jesus buy you back into His family today.

— ◇ —

Sermon 35

NEEDED: AN AWAKENING
Isaiah 51:1-2; 9-23; 52:1-12

Introduction:

Zion is a synonym for Israel. It is also a picture of the church, especially the phrase, "daughter of Zion." Isaiah describes the sad and pitiful condition of the sinning, sleeping people of God. These are timeless pictures that apply to the church and to individual believers. There is abundant evidence that Isaiah's cry for an awakening is relevant to our modern condition. Three times across these two chapters the statesman-prophet, Isaiah, calls for a great awakening (Isaiah 51:9, 17; 52:1). The word "awake" means *to awaken from sleep and arouse from inactivity*.

These chapters set forth the terrible plight of God's people under the image of "a captive daughter of Zion" (Isaiah 52:2). The people were enslaved and hungry for spiritual food (51:14). Her hands held the "cup of trembling," a symbol of God's wrath (Isaiah 51:17). She was trampled by her enemies (51:23). Those enemies mocked God (52:5). This "daughter of Zion" was forsaken without anyone to comfort (51:18-20). When you analyze these texts, the application to our day is clear:

1. God's people are asleep and in bondage.

2. God's people are spiritually starving.

3. God's people are being chastened.

4. God's people are being trampled by the devil.

5. God's name is mocked in our society.

6. The church has been forsaken by many of her sons.

The answer to all of this is an awakening. These Scriptures reveal that *AN AWAKENING...*

I. **Is A Return to Faith** (51:1-2, 9-1)

Isaiah calls us to look back to the heritage of faith from whence we came. God carved His people from the rock of faith, and by grace dug them out of the pit of sin.

Isaiah 51:1-2, 9-16 sets forth three mighty acts of God that are both the examples and content of our faith:

1. The call of Abraham - (51:1-2)
    Discovering new direction:

In these verses, Abraham and Sarah are set forth as examples. Abraham did the irrational thing in leaving his home in Ur of the Chaldeas. He and Sarah did the impossible by conceiving a child who became the ancestor of the nation Israel. He believed in the invisible when he was willing to offer Isaac as a sacrifice to God.

2. The Exodus from Egypt - (51:9-11)
    Escaping old bondage:

Here again was a tremendous act of faith as Israel, set free from Egypt, crossed the Red Sea.

3. The Creation - (51:12-16)
    Enjoying life without fear:

A fearful people are called to faith in the creator God. Certainly, the God who made outer space, the earth, and us, can handle those who come against us.

We need to wake up to faith in the power and activity of our God today! He gives us faith to explore the new places He may lead us, to escape from bondage that enslaves us, and to enjoy life without fear that cripples us.

II. **Includes A Recognition of Failure** (51:17-23)

Isaiah begins with a call to faith and then moves to a cry for repentance. The people of God must wake up to the awful condition of much of the church and society.

In Isaiah 51:17, the church is viewed as holding a "cup of trembling." The cup of wine was a sign of joy in Israel, but because of sin, God has a "cup of trembling," representing His wrath.

The verses before us (17-23) seem to indicate a three-fold failure:

1. Failure in the family (17-18)

The text repeatedly mentions the sons as abandoning the forsaken daughter of Zion. The failure to pass on the faith to our children must be confessed. We have thought we could program it, buy it, or hire it done. We have failed.

2. Failure to influence the nation ((19-20)

The sword is over our nation again. Still, the unborn are murdered. Still, pornography pours forth like a filthy river. Still, the drug traffickers profit at the expense of our nation's children. Still, we are not crying out to God.

3. Failure as individuals (21-23)

We have allowed the enemy to walk all over us.

III. **Restores Spiritual Freedom** (52:1-12)

When God's people wake up, the following benefits begin to flow in fullness and freedom:

1. You are free to be all God made you to be (52:1-2)

The once trampled and downtrodden daughter is clean, beautiful, and strong in the Lord. The people of God stand in beauty, ability and liberty.

2. You are free from a sense of worthlessness (52:3).

You will wake up to discover all God made you to be. You sold out cheaply, but God bought you back with His best.

3. You will be free from demonic oppression (52:4-6; 51:13).

The fear of the oppressor will be over! You will be walking the freedom road.

4. You will be free to share the good news (52:7, 10)

Salvation is good news, peace, glad tidings, and good things. You will enjoy sharing what you have really experienced. You will know that "God reigns."

5.   You will be free to enjoy worship (51:11, 52:8-9)

These verses speak of the preachers singing together of God's freedom. Then the people break forth into singing. Everlasting joy and gladness are expressed.

6.   You will be free to move out for God (52:11-12).

Recognizing that God goes before and protects us from those who choose to stay behind gives great courage for the church to march on.

Conclusion:

Listen! it is time to wake-up. Wake up to who you are and who you can be. Wake up to all God is and can be! Wake up to a life of freedom and victory.

— ✧ —

Sermon 36

THE WOUNDS THAT HEAL
Isaiah 53:1-12

Introduction:

This passage is the zenith and apex of prophetic scripture. The Divine's pen describes in crimson letters of blood the awful agony of Christ's crucifixion. Remarkably, the prophetic eye focused sharply upon this event, though it was seven hundred years in the future.

This text is a holy sanctuary we enter with reverence and depart in repentance. No sensitive person can read these words and remain unchanged. They will either prove that you're hardened and in danger of reprobation, or they will prod you to Christ.

This is the fourth of the servant songs of Isaiah (See 42:1-9, 49:1-13, 50:4-10, 52:13-53:12). These passages begin with the phrase "Behold my servant" and anticipate the coming of the Messiah, Jesus Christ.

These foregleams of Christ now come together in a startling portrait! Isaiah 52:13-53:2 set forth the amazing and unexpected appearing of the Messiah. Though Christ's exaltation in the future was certain, His appearance was unexpected. His facial features were marred and His expressions were sorrowful. He came like other men. In the appearance of His flesh, He was unattractive. To look upon Him with the natural eye would not reveal His regal origin. Yet, when we hear the report of Heaven and receive the record of what He has done, then we are drawn to Him in love. Two outstanding thoughts in this passage claim our attention:

I. His Astonishing Passion (53:3-9)

The words of this text are astonishing (vs. 14), startling (vs. 15), and unbelievable (53:1). Who would ever believe that Yahweh would become one of us, and that, as a man,

He would suffer as both the sacrificial lamb and the scapegoat for the sins of the people? We note two things about the sufferings of Jesus.

1. His passion was emotional (53:1-4).

Jesus Christ experienced rejection by His family, His race, His religion, and finally by His Father. This rejection is summed up in the cry, "My God, My God, why has thou forsaken me?"

He is called a man of sorrows. Tears were His insignia. He was the Lord of grief. He wept over souls, over cities, over graves, and finally over the cup of pain our sins brought to His sinless lips. He was the prince of pain and emperor of anguish. He knew the loneliness of abandonment. It is said that "we hid, as it were our faces from Him" (53:3). He heard blasphemy rather than blessing. His open soul was one vast quivering wound.

Jeremiah saw Jesus in Lamentations as He cried, "Is it nothing to you, all you who pass by, behold and see if there be any sorrow like unto my sorrow" (Lamentations 1:12).

> Man of sorrows, what a name,
> For the Son of God who came!
> Ruined sinners to reclaim,
> Hallelujah! What a Savior!

2. His Passion was physical (53:5-9).

In verse 5, the word "wounded" can be better translated *pierced*. Our Lord's hands, feet, and side were pierced on the cross. His body was bruised by the blows of the soldier. He was whipped and His body bore the stripes we deserved.

In verse 6, the word "laid on him" can be translated "were made to meet upon Him." The word indicates that Jesus fulfilled the Old Testament sacrifice of the scapegoat. In Isaiah, two goats were brought to the priest. One was killed and some of its blood placed upon the living goat. Then the priest laid his hands upon the head of the living goat and confessed the sins of the people. The goat was then carried away into the wilderness where it was released and would finally die. This pictured the taking away of the sin of the people.

The Father placed the sin of all the world of all time on

the head of Jesus. He bore our sins away into that uncharted land "as far as the east is from the west," never to be remembered.

In verse 7, Jesus endured the "oppression" of Satan and the spiritual forces of wickedness. He could hear the accusation of fallen Lucifer. He remembers the hateful cry, echoing through the ages, as one third of the angels fell. Now they exact their revenge.

In verse 7, He is seen to be the "slaughtered Lamb." He is the fulfillment of the Passover lamb and the atoning Lamb. His blood will be the final and only acceptable sacrifice for the sin of humanity, fulfilling the promise pictured by the sacrifices of Israel.

Jesus' suffering ended in physical death. Verses 8-9 indicate that Jesus was buried in a rich man's tomb - a prophecy perfectly fulfilled by His burial in the tomb of Joseph of Arimathea.

II. His Amazing Mission (53:10)

The passion of Jesus was not an accident. It was not of human origin. He came on a vital mission—*to die for us.*

1. His mission was planned in *eternity* (vs. 10).

Oh divine mystery! It was the Father's will that He be bruised. In the counsels of eternity, our salvation and its high cost were decreed. Jesus' death was an act of obedience (See Philippians 2).

2. His mission was executed in *history* (vs. 10b).

His soul was an offering for sin. Why did Jesus suffer? As we look back through our text, we can see why. The Scripture tells us that:

"He was wounded for our transgressions." (vs. 5)
"He was bruised for our iniquities." (vs. 5)
"He was chastised for our peace." (vs. 5)
"He was striped for our healing." (vs. 5)
"Our iniquities were laid upon Him." (vs. 6)
"He was stricken for transgressions." (vs. 8)
"His soul was an offering for sin." (vs. 10
"He shall bear their iniquities." (vs. 11)
"He bore the sin of many." (vs. 12)

Who can question the fact that Jesus Christ bore the punishment of sin that was not His own? God sent Jesus to take our nature, to become our sin and to die in our place. To a world that was lost He gave all He could give to save us and give us a reason to live.

Have you been rejected? So has Jesus. Have you known grief and sorrow? So has Jesus. His stripes provide the healing your heart needs. He has endured the pain and punishment that sin brought into the world.

3. His mission was completed in victory (53:10b-12). *First*, Jesus Christ "prolonged His days" (vs. 10b), by being raised from the grave. He won the victory of death!

Second, He received pleasure and satisfaction from those who are being justified by His work (vs. 11).

Third, He has been enjoying His position by dividing the spoils of victory with His children. "He spoiled principalities and powers" (Colossians 2:15), thus Satan has been conquered. He has shared that victory with us. He continues in intercession for us, keeping us in His victory.

Conclusion:

Alexander the Great often marched his Macedonian armies long and torturous distances. Yet, his soldiers never grumbled because Alexander himself would walk with them. Often, he would pass his water ration to a weaker soldier. They bore up under the pain of the journey because they knew he suffered with them.

There is One far greater than Alexander who walked our path. Yet He walked further than we could walk. He went all the way to Calvary for you and for me. "Who has believed our report" (53:1)? Is it too unbelievable? Does it astonish you that Jesus died for you? It may sound *too good to be true*, but this is the truth of the gospel—This is the amazing grace by which we are saved and that causes our hearts to rejoice.

I stand amazed in the presence
Of Jesus the Nazarene,
And wonder how He could love me,
A sinner condemned unclean.

For me it was in the garden,
    He prayed, not My will, but Thine;
He had no tears for His own griefs,
    But sweat drops of blood for mine.

He took my sins and my sorrows,
    He made them His very own;
He bore the burden to Calvary,
    And suffered and died alone.

O how marvelous! O how wonderful,
    And my song shall ever be;
How marvelous, How wonderful
    Is my Savior's love for me!

- copied

— ✧ —

Sermon 37

THE CHURCH TRIUMPHANT
Isaiah 54:1-17

Introduction:

I heard a fable about a man who, along with his young son, led his donkey through a village. The people of the village criticized his stupidity for not riding the donkey. He then mounted and began to ride the donkey. When they got to the next village, he was criticized for his thoughtlessness in not letting the boy ride.

Then the boy got on the donkey and as they passed through the next village, he was criticized for being lazy. Then they both got on the donkey. As they passed through the fourth village, they were accused of cruelty to the animal. This poor man was last seen carrying the donkey!

This silly fable shows the folly of trying to fit into the mold of others. This has been one of the great problems of the church. The church's leadership has tried to be what its constituency, its critics, and its culture said it ought to be. The consequences of all this is—*the church carrying the donkey.* While a few churches thrive (primarily younger churches), most churches are struggling along, losing rather than gaining. Perhaps we have listened too much to our critics and too little to God.

Right in the middle of the second section of Isaiah, which stretches from chapter 40 through 55, we discover a glorious portrait of the *church triumphant.* The setting of these chapters is Israel's return and restoration after the Babylonian captivity. The promises of Isaiah 40-55 include the coming of God's suffering servant to die for the people, His resurrection, the outpouring of His blessing upon the people, and their awakening to the truth. Isaiah 54 pictures the establishment of God's new covenant of peace and it is a wonderful picture of the church revived and triumphant. In this passage, we focus on three areas that reveal the marks of a triumphant church:

185

I.   The Growth of the Church (54:3)

The scene described in these verses is of a bedouin woman who was widowed and childless. She is living in a small tent suitable for her. Suddenly, the news comes to her that she is to be married and have children. She is instructed to enlarge her tent. Her family is to grow and expand. Likewise, the church, as the bride of Christ, has as its joyful function the birth of children!

1.   The growth of the church is an *exciting* experience. Birth is a time of celebration for the family. We sing because we are part of the family and we sing because of the new members of the family.

2.   The growth will be *extensive*. These expressions speak of more land and a bigger tent.

3.   The growth is an *expensive* growth. The instruction is "do not spare." We would say, *spare no expense*. Whatever it takes to make room for the family we must do.

4.   The growth is an *exhaustive* growth. They are not only to "lengthen the cords," they must "strengthen the stakes." The growth is not only wide but deep. No shallow evangelism will do.

5.   The growth is to be *expansive*. This means that the growth will come from every direction and ministry.

6.   The growth is an *expected* growth. We should be like the expectant mother—prepared to receive children.

In Nottingham, England, May 31, 1792, a young Baptist preacher spoke from this text. He was urging missions and soul-winning upon the people. His outline was two-fold, "expect great things from God" and "attempt great things for God." This one sermon launched the world encircling Baptist missionary enterprise. He was William Carey. Said he that day, "I will go into the darkest pit if you will hold the ropes."

II.   The God of the Church (54:4-10)

What is it that causes a church to operate in fearless faith (vs. 4)? It is knowing God—not merely knowing about Him. The following verses reveal some exciting and encouraging things about Him:

1. He is our Maker (vs. 5).
This is the same word found in Genesis 1:7 concerning the creation of the world. The Lord is the one who can rebuild lives and build the church.
2. He is our Husband (vs. 5).
A husband's function in the Bible is to love and lead. Jesus is our lover and leader. No one ever loved you like He loves you.
3. He is the Lord of Hosts (vs. 5).
"Lord" is the covenant name of God. It is Jehovah or Yahweh, meaning "I Am." He is everything we need. The "hosts" are the angel armies that are at His and at our disposal.
4. He is our Redeemer.
This means at infinite cost He has bought you out of slavery and set you free to live as a son in His family!
5. He is the Holy One of Israel (vs 5).
The God we serve is separate and sinless. He is a God who keeps His word.
6. He is the God of the whole earth (vs. 5).
Our God is not limited to one race, one nation, or even one church. He is the Sovereign over the whole earth.

Now, the church is assured of victory. We are married to Jesus Christ. He is our maker, our lover, our Lord, our Redeemer, and our source.

He has called us into a new covenant. His judgments were to correct us. He has summoned us to everlasting kindness (vs. 8) and everlasting peace (vs. 10). He has come with the hosts of angels to aid us in our cause. We need not be afraid—the victory is ours.

III. **The Glory of the Church** (54:11-17)

1. Glory in the midst of fears,
The glory of the church is a sustaining hope when difficulties come. We can be afflicted and storm-tossed (vs. 11). We can be afraid (vs. 14). We can be attacked (vs. 14, 17). What is it that keeps the church moving in this kind of a fearful culture? It is the hope of glory. Glory is the revealed presence and power of God. Glory is God showing Himself

strong on behalf of those who belong to Him.

2.   Glory in the future (vs. 11-19),

We shall exchange our enlarged tent for a city! These jewels are similar to the description found in Revelation 20:9-27. Jesus is building the church here and the city there!

The fiery blue sapphire is the foundation.   In other texts, Jehovah stands on the sapphire; it is the fifth stone in the high priest's breast plate; it is the second foundation of the new Jerusalem.   Symbolically, the blue represents faithful love.   The underpinnings of all the church is the faithful love of God.

The blood-red ruby pinnacles represent the blood of Jesus as the watch towers of that city.

The gates, called crystal or agate, could be pearl. Nevertheless, quartz crystal or agate or pearls are all formed through pressure or suffering.   It is the suffering of our Lord that opens the gates of that city!

3.   Glory in the fight (14-17),

The devil and his hordes cannot oppress the church unless we allow it.   These demonic terrorists have no right to afflict the church (vs. 14-15).   Look at the great promise of verse 17, "no weapon formed against you shall prosper." The church need not fear, for we shall share His glory.

Conclusion:

Are you a part of the church, a part of His covenant people? If not, you can be.   You enter in through faith in Christ.   Would you receive Him now, trusting in His death on calvary as payment for your sin?   As you do this, you are born again.

— ✧ —

Sermon 38

THE GREAT INVITATION
Isaiah 55:1-13

Introduction:

In the near and middle eastern lands, much day to day exchange still takes place in the bazaars. You can walk through the old city of Jerusalem and you will find yourself besieged by skillful barkers.

The scene in our text is clear. Jehovah has opened a store in the marketplace. There, like a street vendor, He calls for those passing by to come for water, wine and milk. Money cannot buy Jehovah's products. Yet the customer is exhorted to buy without money.

The three products offered are water, wine and milk. Water always represents life. It symbolizes the word of God. Its consumption is a picture of salvation. Its cleansing quality represents regeneration. Water is a symbol of the fullness of the Spirit. Its mighty force at flood tide demonstrates the powerful flow of revival.

Wine in the Old Testament represented three qualities. The first was abundant joy. The second was ceremonial. The cup was a part of their worship, especially at Passover. The blood of the grape represented the blood of sacrifice that pointed to the coming of the Messiah, Jesus. The third was medicinal. Wine was both an anesthetic to ease pain and an antiseptic poured into the wound.

Thus, Jehovah's offer is clearly an offer of salvation, cleansing, and the fullness of the Holy Spirit. This is to be received with joy and celebration and will bring health and healing as promised in Isaiah 53:5-6.

After receiving these benefits, the person is ready to be fed the milk of the Word. The Bible is called the "sincere milk of the word." This is the promise of spiritual growth. "Bread" is the staff of life. Jesus describes Himself as "the bread of life." All of this points to growth. Note first:

189

I. **The Offer of Heaven** (55:1-5)

God stands in the marketplace of man with His five-fold offer:

1.   What money can't buy (vs. 2),

Money is useful but not eternal. There are some temporal things money can do, but it can't buy the deepest, lasting needs of the human heart.

Jay Gould was a rich man and a national leader early in this century. He had everything materially, but he said, "I suppose I am the most miserable man on earth." In the end, only a relationship with God through Christ can satisfy.

2.   What labor can't earn (vs. 2),

Man often works hard because he wants more. Often we labor so that we can enjoy. We live in a T.G.I.F. society. We labor to live on the weekends. Our society is entertainment mad.

My two favorite poets are Tennyson and Burns. The great Scot Burns wrote about pleasure:

> But pleasures are like poppies spread,
>   You seize the flower, its bloom is shed;
> Or like the snow falls in the river,
>   A moment white—then melts forever;
> Or like the rainbow's lovely form,
>   Arising amid the storm.

There are very few survivors of the mad pace of pleasure. The laughter, the liquor, and the luxuries; and the playthings, pleasures, and possessions are surface scratches to an itch that is heart deep!

3.   What death can't cancel (vs. 3),

When we trust the Lord, it is our "soul" that enjoys the quality of eternal life now.

4.   What failure cannot forfeit (vs. 3),

Here we are promised an everlasting contract according to the "sure mercies of David." You remember David the shepherd boy who slew Goliath. The leader, forged in the weariness of the wilderness, the man who went after the heart of God, restoring praise and worship to the people, by bringing the throne of God (the ark of the covenant) back to Jerusalem—This monarch fell into most grievous sin! He committed adultery and plotted murder for his own pleasure! Yet, God forgave him. God had made an everlasting arrangement with David. God's contract with you is irrevocable. Your failure will not forfeit what your works could never earn! Beloved, failure cannot forfeit the salvation of God. God offers that which time cannot tarnish (vs. 4-5). As the years pass by and the witness of Christ is given, the splendor and glory of it shines more brilliantly.

The Islamic religion with its "man can earn it or go to hell" philosophy can only spread through ignorance and fear. The shadow of the New Age religion offers nothing the soul can hold onto. The simple message of Jesus, pardon and salvation, shines more gloriously than ever today. Note secondly:

II. **The Opportunity of Humanity** (55:6-13)

Man's opportunity can be grasped in the following four ways:

1. Man must respond (vs. 6).

Verse 7 indicates that man must respond willingly. What one "seeks" must be sought in a timely manner. Now "the Lord is near" and "may be found." The Scripture indicates a limit on man's opportunity. A person may grow hardened as did Pharaoh of Egypt. A person may die as did the rich fool in Luke 15. You could sin away your day of grace as did Belshazzar.

2. Man must repent (vs. 7).

Here is the clearest definition of real repentance in all of the Bible! The repentant sinner changes direction and goes another way. The repentant sinner is changed on the inside. The thought life is cleaned up. Some of you are sinners in your thinking! Repentance is not only turning from sin, it is turning to the Lord. "Lord" means *master*, and *provider*. Life moves under His Lordship.

3. Man must receive (vs. 7).

Our God will have mercy and freely pardon. When man hears this, he cries out, "impossible, too simple, and not the way I would do it." The Lord does not think or act as fallen man. Man breaks promises, God keeps promises. Man remembers and wants revenge. God forgives and forgets. Man wants his "pound of flesh" to quote Shakespeare in the Merchant of Venice. Man wants life by works and God pardons freely.

Man is unfaithful while God is faithful. His Word, like the sown field, will give its harvest. God's word will not return with an empty basket (vs. 8-11).

4. Man will rejoice (vs. 12-13).

Joy and peace will be the heritage of redeemed humanity. All of nature will one day explode in praise to God. In fact the world can sing today for those who can hear.

Conclusion:

Only Jesus can give true satisfaction (vs. 2). He is the true source of a life of purpose. While many are seeking vicarious spiritual experiences offered by New Age dominated entertainment, the real offer of spiritual life is ignored. There is a real God who came and stood in the marketplace of the world and cried "come unto me." He cried it from a cross and on the other side of an empty tomb. He still cries out in the midst of our world. Can you hear Him calling you? Will you respond?

>Only Jesus can satisfy your soul;
>   Only He can change your life
>And make you whole.
>   He'll give you peace, you never knew,
>Sweet love and joy and Heaven too;
>   Only Jesus can satisfy your soul.

>- Lanny Wolfe

— ✧ —

Sermon 39

THE DIVINE DISCIPLINES
Isaiah 56:6-8; 57:14-21; 58:6-12;
59:16-19

Introduction:

John Keats, the English poet, was right when he said,
"Nothing ever becomes real till it is experienced." We live
in a day when the Christian life is taught in seminars and
preached from the pulpit, yet few actually experience the
living of it.

Authentic Christianity is not formal, denominational or
organizational. Genuine Christianity is spiritual. It is
heart and soul deep! You cannot be an authentic Christian
and run with the pace, pressures and pleasures of this
world. You can be a surface Christian, but your life will
lack the touch and power of the supernatural.

The genuine Christian's character is deeper, spirit is
gentler, courage is stronger and conviction is clearer. His
relationship with Jesus has the fire of love and passion, and
he sticks to his commitments.

These four chapters are sandwiched between God's call
to a covenant relationship. In Isaiah 56:4-6, the believer is
called to "hold fast" the covenant. In Isaiah 59:21, God
again promises a covenant that will stretch across many
generations. This is a call to a lasting commitment to the
Lord.

What is the secret of success in the Christian life? God
gives us clear disciplines that will enable us to experience
a genuine spiritual life. Only a genuine Christian life can
make you an authentic Christian. The authentic Christian
will have a life and witness that ring true before a watching
world. The secret to such a life is in the disciplines of the
Christian life. Disciples are those who gather around Jesus
and do the things He does.

Woven in the fabric of these four chapters of Isaiah

under the theme of *covenant* are four divine disciplines of authentic faith.

I. The Discipline of Prayer (56:6-8)

We find three things about prayer in these verses:

1. Notice first that prayer is a corporate responsibility. Prayer is a ministry for all in God's house. It is this passage that Jesus cited when He cleansed the temple. The money changers and animal sellers had set up shop in the court of the Gentiles (non-Jewish nations). The Lord was angry when prayer could not be offered in His house.

2. Prayer in God's house is offered with joyful praise. The Lord promises to make us joyful as we gather in, not away from, His house to pray.

3. Prayer is evangelistic. God promises to bring in others when we are faithful in intercession.

II. The Discipline of Humility (57:14-15)

Isaiah reveals the number one stumbling block before his people (57:14). That stumbling block is pride. Humility is the opposite of pride. It is laying one's life before God. It is a submission before God. The humble are those who recognize their position before the great God of the universe. God is High and Holy. He fills all of the ages of eternity.

Our God who dwells in heaven also promises to dwell with those who are willing to go down before Him in submission and repentance. God has promised to heal, lead and comfort those who are willing to acknowledge their need before Him. As long as we are self-sufficient, God will not heal us or our land.

III. The Discipline of Fasting (58:6-12)

Fasting is going without food and pleasures for a season. It is a discipline that God honors for the accomplishing of special objectives in prayer:

1. To break the power of sin in the life of another "loose the bonds of wickedness" (58:6),

2. To assist those under crushing burdens - "undo heavy burdens" (58:6),

3. To deal with the demonic - "to let the oppressed go free" (58:6),
4. To create concern and give aid to the needy (58:7),
5. To begin anew with God (58:8),
6. To bring healing (58:8),
7. To experience the glory of God (58:8),
8. To bring answer to prayer (58:9),
9. To gain clear guidance and provision from God (58:11),
10. To repair and restore families and civilizations (58:12).

IV. The Discipline of Spiritual Warfare (59:16-19)

Believers who are clothed in the armor of God (Ephesians 6:10-18) and are willing to stand in the gap for the souls of others are called intercessors (vs. 16). God is amazed that believers do not care for the captive and dying. When the church in praying, submits to Jesus in self-denial, then God clothes them with power. The Spirit of God will lift up a standard against the enemy (vs. 19). That "standard" is the people of God. God will lift up His church and say to all of the kingdom of evil, "See my people; they live out my life!

Conclusion:

What can happen when individuals in covenant with the church get serious about their devotional lives? What happens when we take our responsibility as God's intercessors and God's banner seriously? God will send revival. Satan will be in retreat. Captives will be set free. The gospel will be received.

— ✧ —

Sermon 40

LIGHT FOR DAYS OF DARKNESS
Isaiah 60:1-5; 19-20

Introduction:

Here in the hills of East Tennessee, autumn brings beautiful and unusual weather. Often the moisture from the Gulf of Mexico collides with the cold sweeping down from the north. This results in a drizzle and fog in the early morning hours. As the day progresses, the light and heat of the sun, ninety-three million miles away, begins to penetrate and burn off the morning moisture, revealing the brilliant autumn colors.

Isaiah views history with such a metaphor. The earth is viewed as being shrouded in darkness and the people in even deeper darkness. This darkness symbolizes the seemingly hopeless condition of our world and its people. Isaiah's words reflect the hope of ancient Israel and the hope of the world.

When one reads these closing chapters of Isaiah, hope rises in the heart. In his *PARACELSUS*, Robert Browning said "We are the heirs of hopes too fair to turn out false."

Darkness in Scripture symbolizes many distressing truths. In the ancient creation account, God's first word over a chaotic creation was, "Let there be light" (Genesis 1:3). Darkness is viewed as hostile to the light (John 1:5). It symbolizes the dominion of the devil (Colossians 1:13). Darkness is an evil empire from which humanity needs deliverance.

Darkness stands for the place of all who hate good (John 3:18-21). Men love darkness because it hides the heinous evil of their lives.

Darkness represents ignorance of the truth. People without Christ walk in darkness (John 8:12).

Finally, darkness represents death, hell and judgement. Hell is called "outer darkness."

When we view with unprejudiced eyes our society,

197

illuminated by the light of God, we see Satan on the throne, moral corruption, ignorance, and impending judgement.

Is light of human decency so low that baby killing can be thought to be someone's right or choice? Can we continue to allow sexual perversion to be paraded as normal? Are times so dark that anything goes in our nation. Is the darkness so dark that we no longer know good from evil?

There is hope! Israel faced captivity and punishment for her moral and spiritual failures. In the midst of all that, God promised light! This promise extends to all of us today, but how can we switch on the light in days of darkness?

I. **You Must Receive the Light**.

"Arise." Receiving the light begins when you are sick and tired of darkness. Repentance is the need. The call of Isaiah is to action. "Arise," get up and move out of the darkness. This word is used not only for a sunrise, but as a word for resurrection from the dead. Malachi 4:2 speaks of our Lord, "But to you who reverence my name, the sun of righteousness shall arise with healing in His wings." Ephesians 2:1-10 likens salvation to being raised from the dead. John 1:4 says of Jesus, "In Him was life and the life was the light of men."

When you open your heart to Jesus Christ, then your blindness is at an end. Light has come into your life. Truths you never understood become clear to you. Sins you never thought so bad become hateful to you. Confusion leaves and clear direction begins to come.

God has three sources of illumination that flow from Him. His Son, Jesus, is the Light of the World. Secondly, His Word is spoken of as light. "Thy word is a lamp unto my feet and light unto my path." "The entrance of thy word giveth light." The third source of light is God's people. We can see Jesus in others.

II. **You Need to Reflect the Light**. 60:2-3).

"His glory will be seen upon you" (60:3). A lamp burns but a mirror shines. The light of Jesus comes upon us, within us, and at last it shines from us. In Matthew 5:14, Jesus said, "You are the light of the world." The church is

God's lampstand in a dark world. Our lives need to reflect the life of Jesus Christ. Such is the life of Robert Reed. Listen to his story as told by Max Lucado:

"I have everything I need for joy!" Robert Reed said. "Amazing!" I thought! His hands are twisted and his feet are useless. He can't bathe himself. He can't feed himself. He can't brush his teeth, comb his hair, or put on his underwear. His shirts are held together by strips of velcro. His speech drags like a worn-out audio cassette. Robert has cerebral palsy.

The disease keeps him from driving a car, riding a bike, and going for a walk. But it didn't keep him from graduating from high school or attending Abilene Christian University, from which he graduated with a degree in Latin. Having cerebral palsy didn't keep him from teaching at a St. Louis junior college or from venturing overseas on five mission trips. And, Robert's disease didn't prevent him from becoming a missionary in Portugal.

He moved to Lisbon, alone, in 1972. There, he rented a hotel room and began studying Portuguese. He found a restaurant owner who would feed him after the rush hour and a tutor who would instruct him in the language. Then he stationed himself daily in a park, where he distributed brochures about Christ. Within six years he led seventy people to the Lord, one of whom became his wife, Rosa.

I heard Robert speak recently. I watched other men carry him in his wheelchair onto the platform. I watched them lay a Bible in his lap. I watched his stiff fingers force open the pages. And I watched people in the audience wipe away tears of admiration from their faces. Robert could have asked for sympathy or pity, but he did just the opposite. He held his bent hand up in the air and boasted, "I have everything I need for joy." His shirts are held together by velcro, but his life is held together by joy."

III. **You Should Respond to the Light**. (60:2-3).

The word "arise" is generally connected to another action word. Nehemiah used the word to stir the people to "arise and build." God used the word to call Jonah to "arise and go." Isaiah used it to stir the people from their unbelief to "arise and shine."

We are to:

1. Work while it is light (John 9:4).
2. War against evil while there is light (Rom. 13:12).
3. Walk in the light (Ephesians 5:8).
4. Witness in the light (Philippians 2:13).
5. Watch in the light (I Thessalonians 5:5-6).

IV. **You Should Rejoice in the Light** (60:5, 15-21).

This passage proclaims the millennial future of Israel: A day when the nation is restored spiritually, when other nations befriend them, when man turns to Jehovah Jesus as their God, and when peace comes. This will happen when Jesus sits again on the throne of Israel after His return.

Yet, on whatever heart He is enthroned today, these benefits are available. He promises to meet our needs, to glorify His house, to protect us, and to bring peace to us. He also includes all of us Gentiles in His promise of the future kingdom. He will be our everlasting light" (Isaiah 60:19-20).

The Bible says, "Then will your heart throb with joy." (Isaiah 60:5). Ours is the joy of living and the joy of dying. He is our light now and He will be our light then.

Conclusion:

Two men were contemporaries, Dwight L. Moody, the evangelist and Robert Ingersoll, the atheist. Said Ingersoll of Christianity, "The Christian creed is the ignorant past bullying the enlightened present." Where was Ingersoll's "enlightened present" when the dark shroud of death descended over his soul. Read the record as follows.

"Ingersoll died suddenly. The news of his death stunned his family. His body was kept at home for several days because his wife was reluctant to part with it. It was eventually removed for the sake of the family's health.

Ingersoll's remains were cremated, and the public response to his passing was altogether dismal. For a man who put all his hopes on this world, death was tragic and came without the consolation of hope...

Moody's legacy was different. On December 22, 1899, Moody awoke to his last winter dawn. Having grown increasingly weak during the night, he began to speak in slow measured words. 'Earth recedes, Heaven opens before me!' His son, Will, who was near by, hurried across the room to his father's side.

'Father, you are dreaming,' he said. 'No, this is no dream, Will,' Moody said. 'It is beautiful. It is like a trance. If this is death, it is sweet. God is calling me, and I must go. Don't call me back.'

At that point, the family gathered around, and moments later the great evangelist died. It was his coronation day, a day he had looked forward to for many years. He was with his Lord.

The funeral service of Dwight L. Moody reflected that same confidence. There was no despair. Loved ones gathered to sing praise to God at a triumphant home-going service. Many remembered the words the evangelist had spoken earlier that year in New York City: 'Someday you will read in the papers that Moody is dead. Don't you believe a word of it. At that moment I shall be more alive than I am now....I was born of the flesh in 1837, I was born of the Spirit in 1855. That which is born of the flesh may die. That which is born of the Spirit shall live forever.'"

Faith in Christ is not a *leap into the dark*, but a *walk into the light*.

— ✧ —

Sermon 41

HOW TO KNOW REAL FREEDOM
Isaiah 61:1-11

Introduction:

Jesus preached His first sermon in Nazareth at His home church. His text was Isaiah 61:1-2. When he finished the sermon, the listeners tried to kill Him because they heard Him say, "The Spirit of the Lord is upon me, because he hath anointed me to preach the gospel to the poor; he hath sent me to heal the brokenhearted, to preach deliverance to the captives, and recovering of sight to the blind, to set at liberty them that are bruised, To preach the acceptable year of the Lord." And he closed the book, and he gave it again to the minister, and sat down. And the eyes of all them who were in the synagogue were fastened on him. And he began to say unto them, "This day is this scripture fulfilled in your ears" (Luke 4:18-21). When Jesus said that, He identified Himself as the Messiah.

This passage is the *document of liberty* for all who will believe. In the islands of the Caribbean, the institution of slavery was finally broken. At midnight, a coffin filled with chains was buried, symbolizing the death of slavery. When Jesus made this proclamation, it was the death knell for the spiritual slavery for all humanity. Lincoln issued the *Emancipation Proclamation* in 1863, freeing the slaves in America. It took a war to enforce that edict. Likewise, Jesus has declared war on all that was against mankind.

When we review the prophecy in Isaiah, it is evident that it portrays the benefits of the freedom Jesus came to give—There are five that answer our heart's longing.

I. **Liberty** (vs. 1-2)

Note again, "The Spirit of the Lord God is upon me; because the Lord hath anointed me to preach good tidings

203

unto the meek; he hath sent me to bind up the brokenhearted, to proclaim liberty to the captives, and the opening of the prison to them that are bound; To proclaim the acceptable year of the Lord, and the day of vengeance of our God; to comfort all that mourn."

The Lord was the "anointed" One. This word translates the Hebrew, *massa,* which is a root of Messiah. Why did the Messiah come? Our text tells us clearly. He came to bring good news to the meek. The meek are the toil worn, the helpless, and those without rights or recourse. He brought good news to those whom life has worn out.

The brokenhearted are those whose hearts have been shattered. The Hebrew word "shabhar" means *to break beyond use.* It is the word used of ships broken up by a storm. Jesus came to put the broken heart together again.

He came to break the bondage that keeps us from being all we can be. He came to open the dark dungeon of despair and lead us into the light. He came to say that God will accept all who will accept His Messiah. He is our liberator.

The Jews observed a Biblical custom called Jubilee. It was the fiftieth year occurring at the end of seven sabbatical cycles of seven years each, in which all land was returned to its ancestral owners and all Israelite slaves were freed. The Jubilee is described in Leviticus 25:8-17, 23-55; 27:16--25; and Numbers 36:4. It was proclaimed with the blowing of the shophar, a trumpet made from a ram's horn, on the Day of Atonement. (Hebrew, *yovel* - "Jubilee," takes its name from the ram's horn.) We can now rejoice that through the atoning blood of our Savior we are free and our inheritance is restored.

II. Beauty (vs. 3)

"To console them who mourn in Zion, to give them beauty for ashes, the oil of joy for mourning, the garment of praise for the spirit of heaviness; that they might be called trees of righteousness, the planting of the Lord, that He might be glorified."

What a wonderful promise! The mourners put ashes on their heads and bodies. God promises beauty for the burned puts to flight the spirit of heaviness. The depression that many of you experience can be healed through praise. That is why I am leading our church into freer praise where the spirit of heaviness can be cast out. Jesus has come, in the words of Bill Gaither, "to make something beautiful of your life." Olive oil was applied to the face and hair to make it shine and it was spicy to give off a sweet fragrance. The anointing of the Spirit put on us a glow and fragrance of heaven.

I remember walking into a restaurant and a beautiful young girl running over and embracing me. I did not recognize her because she did not look like the scuffy teenage girl I had begged a New Orleans judge not to send to jail. The beauty of the Lord had changed her life.

III. **Ability** (vs. 4-5)

"And they shall rebuild the old ruins; they shall raise up the former desolations, and they shall repair the ruined cities, the desolations of many generations. And strangers shall stand and feed your flocks, and the sons of the foreigner shall be your plowmen and your vinedressers."

God promises to set you free in order to accomplish something through you. We are to build, to raise up, and to repair. When the Lord sets you free, then He puts you in the business of reclaiming wasted lives, restoring that which has been left desolate and empty. A home that once rang with laughter and love but now is desolate because of sin, Jesus can repair. Society and our posterity can be changed and those changes will reach far into the future. There is no limit to what God can do through you.

IV. **Identity** (vs. 6)

"But you shall be named the Priests of the Lord: they shall call you the servants of our God: you shall eat the riches of the Gentiles, and in their glory you shall boast."

In verses 3 and 6, there is a threefold description of the free people of God:

 1. Trees of Righteousness

The word "tree" in Hebrew is *terebinth* which is the oak. The free believer can stand tall and strong in the righteousness of Christ.

 2. Priests of the Lord

This means that every believer has access to God without going through anyone but Jesus.

 3. Servants of God

This means ministers of God. All of the saved are *somebodies* in the Kingdom of God. Your life has significance with Christ.

V. **Prosperity** (vs. 7-9)

"Instead of your shame you shall have double honor, and instead of confusion they shall rejoice in their portion. Therefore, in their land they shall possess double; Everlasting joy shall be theirs. For I, the Lord, love justice, I hate robbery for burnt offering; I will direct their work in truth, and I will make with them an everlasting covenant. Their descendants shall be known among the Gentiles, and their offspring among the people. All who see them shall acknowledge them. That they are the posterity whom the Lord hath blessed."

True prosperity is not simply having wealth. Some of the saddest and most miserable people are affluent. These verses give us the three marks of true prosperity:

 1. True prosperity is the ability to enjoy what you have regardless of the amount.

 2. It is also the testimony that you keep your word because God keeps His. When life is over, will you be remembered as one who kept the faith as the Apostle Paul did?

 3. Also, true prosperity is leaving your family blessed and not cursed.

Conclusion:

Jesus came to set you free to be all you can possibly be. How can you experience this freedom?

Note vs. 10-11. "I will greatly rejoice in the Lord, my soul shall be joyful in my God; for He hath clothed me with the garments of salvation, He hath covered me with the robe of righteousness, as a bridegroom decks himself with ornaments, and as a bride adorns herself with her jewels.

For as the earth bringeth forth its bud, and as the garden causes the things that are sown in it to spring forth; so the Lord God will cause righteousness and praise to spring forth before all the nations."

In these closing verses, the pronoun changes from "they" to "I." Here is what an individual can do.

1. Receive salvation - Christ *for* you.
2. Wear the Robe of Righteousness - Christ *in* you. The righteousness of Jesus replaces our rags.
3. Grow into a fruitful Christian - Christ *through* you.

— ✧ —

Sermon 42

FINDING THE LOVE OF YOUR LIFE
Isaiah 62:1-12

Introduction:

In *MY FAIR LADY* you have the story of a poor, uneducated girl who is utterly transformed into a lady and, eventually, a bride. This theme is an old romantic idea that began with the play, *PYGMALION,* and is now the theme of the rather dubious imitator, *PRETTY WOMAN.* The Bible is filled with romance. Rahab, a prostitute, became the bride of an ancestor of David, as does the Moabitess widow, Ruth. Who can forget the heroic story of Esther whose elevation from captive to queen made it possible to save her nation?

The greatest romance in all the Bible is the pursuit of humanity by the great God of Love who came in Jesus Christ. People want to be loved and they seek love, as the country song says, "in all the wrong places." The truth is—the One you long for is seeking you.

Our text throbs and pulsates with the excitement of love and romance. The people of God, symbolized by the bride and city, are viewed as the objects of the ardent love of God. In our text, we see the *proposal,* the *preparation,* and the *prospect* of the bride of the Lord.

I. The Proposal to the Bride (62:1-5)

Here we read the promises of God to His beloved. Our Lord brightens life (vs. 1-2a). He removes the dark stains of sin. He destroys the dark shadows of death. He brings light into our lives. He restores the fire of passion. He makes our lives burning lamps that show forth His glory. He gives us purpose in life.

Our Lord renames us. In our text, the people were called "Forsaken" and "Desolate." The new name that the Lord gives is, "Hephzibah, and your land, Beulah: for the

209

Lord delights in you, and your land shall be married" (vs. 4). The word "name" in scripture means *character, family, position* and *identity*. The new name here means *delight* and *marriage*. Marriage confers the name of the bridegroom to the bride. The Lord's name and all it means becomes our name. We receive His character, move into His family, receive a new position, and assume a new identity.

In the Old Testament, Abram and Sarai became Abraham and Sarah. Jacob became Israel. In the New Testament, Simon became Peter and Saul became Paul. These changes indicated a change in status and destiny. The childless patriarch became the father of many nations. The shifty and sinful Jacob became Israel, God's prince. The vacillating Simon became Peter, the Rock. The legalistic Saul became the apostle of grace to the ends of the earth. Look at your own life. You are not what you were before you met Christ.

The Lord rejoices over His bride (vs. 4a-5). Can you see the Lord Jesus like a young bridegroom filled with the joy of the wedding day. It makes Jesus happy when people come to Him and receive His love.

II. The Preparation of the Bride (62:6-10)

In Israel, the proposal was followed by a period of waiting during which the groom and bride would make necessary preparation. The groom would go to prepare a place for a home on his family's estate. The bride would make herself ready for the move to the new home, while her family prepared the celebration to receive the returning bridegroom (See John 14, Matthew 25, Revelation 19:7). Study carefully the preparation Isaiah calls for.

First, the church as bride must bombard Heaven with prayer (vs. 6-8). God has sworn that we shall be called to the marriage supper of the Lamb. We are under the protection of His Word until all His promise is fulfilled.

Second, we must evangelize (vs. 10). We are to go outside the gates of our church and make a highway for others to come into the family. We must remove every rock that might hinder the journey of others to the wedding. We are to lift up a banner to the ends of the earth. The Hebrew for *ensign* is often rendered *banner.* It is usually employed to designate a rallying *standard.*

In Isaiah 11:12, the Messiah is said to raise up such a standard, while verse 10 says that He is Himself one. Perhaps this latter reference is intended to be a link with, "The Lord is my banner" (Jehovah-nissi) in Exodus 17:15. In this account, Moses had his hands held high by Aaron and Hur while the battle raged against the Amalekites. After the victory, Moses built an altar and named it, "The Lord Is my Banner." Our task in preparing for the wedding in heaven is to lift up the Lord as our banner.

III. The Prospect of the Bride (62:11-12)

The glorious prospect of the bride is the coming of the bridegroom. Our text declares that He is coming to claim His people from the ends of the earth. What a glorious proclamation, "Indeed the Lord has proclaimed, To the end of the world: Say to the daughter of Zion, 'Surely your salvation is coming; Behold, His reward is with Him, And His work is before Him'" (vs. 11).

The prepositions, "with" and "before" cause us to focus on two outstanding truths in this verse. When our "salvation" (Jesus) comes:

1. His reward will be with Him.

According to Paul, believers' rewards will be given at the Judgment Seat of Christ. This is the "bema," the seat from which rewards are issued (II Corinthians 5:10).

Paul tells us in I Corinthians 3:9-15 that our works will be tried and revealed for what they are, and our rewards will be issued accordingly. Many will be disappointed, while others will be filled with joyful praise.

Back in Isaiah 62:3, our Lord speaks of crowns and diadems. His people are the crowns of His glory. The New Testament speaks of crowns for the believers. The greatest reward will be seeing Jesus.

2. His work will be before Him.

What a glorious prospect! "And they shall call them the Holy People, The redeemed of the Lord; And you shall be called, Sought Out, A city not forsaken" (vs. 12).

In Adam, we were sold under sin, gone astray, no longer a people, but scattered and battered in a lost world. At the coming of the Bridegroom, our salvation, we will be caught up before Him and we, His work, will be before Him. —revealed as Holy People, Redeemed of the Lord, and Sought Out—all the work of His grace and power.

Conclusion:

This message cries loudly, "Jesus loves me." Dr. Richard Selzer in his book, *MORTAL LESSONS*, gives this narrative:

I stand by the bed where a young woman lies, her face postoperative, her mouth twisted in palsy, clownish. A tiny twig of the facial nerve, the one to the muscles of her mouth, has been severed. This surgeon had followed with religious fervor the curve of her flesh; I promise you that. Nevertheless, to remove the tumor in her cheek, I had cut the little nerve.

Her young husband is in the room. He stands on the opposite side of the bed, and together they seem to dwell in the evening lamplight, isolated from me, private.

"Who are they," I ask myself, "he and this wrymouth I have made, who gaze at and touch each other so generously, greedily?"

The young woman speaks. "Will my mouth always be like this?" she asks. "Yes," I say, "it will." "It is because the nerve was cut."

She nods, and is silent. But the young man smiles. "I like it," he says. "It's kind of cute."

At once I know who he is; I understand—I lower my gaze. Unmindful, he bends to kiss her crooked mouth. I am so close I can see how he twists his own lips to accommodate hers, to show her that their kiss still works."

That's what Jesus did for us. He made His kiss of love fit our twisted lives.

— ✧ —

Sermon 43

WHEN SURRENDER IS VICTORY
Isaiah 63:1-6

Introduction:

Edom, the descendants of Esau and also known as Idumeans, was the ancient enemy of Israel. Their deepening hatred of Israel dates back to the conflict between their father, Esau, and Jacob. Numbers 20:14-21 records the Edomite's refusal of passage of the journeying Israelites through their land. Perpetually Edom was the ally of Israel's enemies. Ezekiel 35:5-6 describes Edom as Israel's ancient enemy who shed the blood of their children. Psalm 137 records the laughter and mocking of Edom when Israel was taken captive by Babylon. In Isaiah's day, Edom was known for its attacks on the Southern border of Israel. Edom would cross the border to spoil the fields, steal the possessions, and murder the unwary Jews.

For this reason, some writers believe that this prophecy speaks of Judas Macabeus who would defeat the Edomites and stop their border terror. Others have said that this warrior is simply a figurative champion of Israel. One writer said it was Jehovah, but not the Messiah. We believe that the Messiah is Jehovah.

There is no question in my mind as to the identity of this crimsoned-clad conqueror. This is a typical prophetic portrait of the Lord Jesus Christ!

There is some disagreement as to what event is specifically prophesied by this passage. Some believe it is a picture of His *passion* while others believe it portrays His *parousia*. I believe both, His cross and His coming, are here proclaimed. Both are times of conquest by our Savior. They are bound together. Golgotha's victory is the guarantee of Armageddon's triumph. Jesus had to be *Mediator* before He could be the *Monarch*. Note three pictures of conquest in this passage: *The conquest of:*

213

I.   **Calvary - The Typical Fulfillment** 63:1a-2)

I am amazed that the writer had to ask "Who is this?" Yet we should not be so startled. Most of Israel did not recognize Him.

In Matthew 21:1-11, we see the account of our Lord's triumphant entry into Jerusalem. Jesus rode into town on a foal of a donkey exactly as Zechariah 9:9 had predicted and on the very day that Daniel 9 had predicted, yet most of the people responded by saying, "Who is this" (Matthew 21:11). Jesus, weeping, said, "If you had known, even you, especially in this your day, the things that make for your peace" (Luke 19:42). "...because you did not know the time of your visitation" (Luke 19:44).

Paul cried out after fifteen years of serving our blessed Lord, "that I might know Him." He wanted to know Jesus more and more. After serving Jesus, I still discover that He is more wonderful every day.

They did not know that the great Jehovah had stooped to become man and die for them. Look at this conqueror from Calvary:

1.   His approach

He is coming from Bozrah, Edom the accursed place. This is typical of this earth where every garden has a thorn, every city a cemetery, and every person, sooner or later, a broken heart.

He has been face to face with our undying and ancient enemies—sin, death and Satan. In John 10:10, Jesus said of Satan, "The thief cometh but for to kill, to steal, and to destroy but I am come that you might have life." Our Lord is viewed here as returning from the realms of darkness and death. He is a returning conqueror.

2.   His apparel

The passage describes His apparel as crimson and glorious. As we look at His appearance, we get a clue as to the struggle He has been through. Why is your clothing red? Jesus answers, "I have been down to the capitol city of the cursed to pay the penalty for your sins. I have been down to grapple with your foe, Satan. I have been down to receive in my body the sting of death you deserve."

I believe that it was in shedding His own blood that our enemies' blood was shed. The commentators rightly point out that the blood at the end of this passage is the blood of the defeated enemies. However, it was His shed blood that smote our enemies. It was His blood that routed hell and crushed our enemies. He is covered in crimson by His conquest of evil.

Look at the battle of our Beloved! Behold our Hero covered with the bloody sweat of Gethsemane. He does not flinch from the fight. How sharp were the swords of our sin that wounded Him. How terrible the blades that sheathed themselves in His body and mind. See His head bleeding with the thorns, His back ripped by the whistling lash, see Him surrounded by the hordes of hell's evil invincible empire.

Hear the cry of the conqueror, "It is finished." See the adversary hurled headlong into hell. The battle does not end there, for our Lord stalks death into its own dark abode. He will not stop until he has, in the words of Colossians 2, "spoiled principalities and powers." He will not stop until He has broken the scepter of sin and sent the monster, death, whimpering into the corner like a whipped puppy. He will not stop until He has kindled the star of the resurrection in the dark vaults of death and come out triumphant on the third day! Yes, He is red with the blood stains of Calvary.

> Who is this that comes from Edom,
> All his raiment stained with blood,
> To the slave proclaiming freedom,
> Bringing and bestowing good?
> Glorious is the garb he wears,
> Glorious is the spoils he bears.

II. Conversion - The Personal Fulfillment (63:1b-3a)

At the end of verse 1 and at the beginning of verse 3, there are two statements that apply personally to all. There must be a personal conquest and surrender in our lives as individuals. Our knees must bow before the conquering Christ. Salvation is a surrender of our lives to Christ.

1.   He speaks (1b).

Our Lord comes speaking in righteousness. Salvation comes to us by the Word of God. The Word of God is described in Hebrews 4 as the Sword of the Spirit. When the Holy Spirit wielded that Sword in our hearts, it made possible our salvation. It is the heavenly scalpel by which we get a heart transplant from Heaven.

2.   He alone saves (3a).

The Lord Jesus had to go alone into the battle. In Revelation 5:4-5, John wept much because no redeemer could be found, Then suddenly the elders say, "Weep not, behold the Lion of the tribe of Judah." Acts 4:12 is still true, "There is none other name given among men by which we must be saved." Now is the time to bow before the Lord Jesus Christ. He is the only Savior.

During the civil war, a dramatic battle called the Battle of the Crater was fought in Petersburg, Virginia. The northerners tunneled under the camp of the southern army and planted explosives. They set off the charge which left a huge crater in the ground and many dead. The northern army advanced, assured of an easy victory. They were trapped by the confederate army and forced to retreat into the crater their explosion had made. There, the northern army was defeated. A plaque commemorating the night of that battle says, "On this night a tragic defeat was turned into a glorious victory."

That could be written about my life and yours. On the cross, where Satan exploded everything he had, our defeats are turned to victory. Note then as Paul says, "We are more than conquerors through Him that loved us" (Romans 8:37-39).

III. **Consummation - The Final Fulfillment** (63:3b-6)

This prophecy moves from victory to victory. Because He was *crucified* on Mt. Calvary, there will be a *coronation* on Mt. Zion. This prophecy is finally fulfilled in Revelation 19:11-16. Verses 4-6 speak of the three purposes of His second coming. *First*, to redeem and rescue His people from this earth; *Second*, to bring retribution on those who do not know Him; *Third*, to reign as Lord over all.

Conclusion:

Look up, dear friend, we are on the victor's side. In the dark hour that comes to all of us, remember that the decisive victory has already been won! The greater battle of the war of 1812 was fought after the war was over. American leaders could not get word to Andrew Jackson in time to stop the Battle of New Orleans. We, however, have a clear word from our Lord, "It is finished."

> I often think I hear His footsteps,
> Stealing down the paths of time;
> And the future dark with shadows,
> Brighter with this hope sublime;
> Sound the soul-inspiring anthem;
> Angel hosts, your harp attune;
> Earth's long night is almost gone;
> Christ is coming, coming soon.

— ✧ —

Sermon 44

WHAT YOUR HEART LONGS FOR
Isaiah 64:1-8; 65:8-25

Introduction:

What do human beings really need? For what do our restless hearts long? One has well said, "There is a God shaped hole in every heart." We may try to fill our hearts with a thousand pursuits and pleasures; yet, they remain gnawingly empty. Augustine said, "Thou hast made us for Thyself and our hearts are restless until they rest in Thee." Every human being has basic needs beyond the physical. Man is innately a spiritual creature and will worship at some altar. What man really needs is a relationship with the living God.

In our text, the prophet expresses his heart's desire for God to come down. In these two chapters, Isaiah has captured the heart cry of every honest person. We need the Lord. In Christ, God has come down to us. Isaiah foresees the attributes of God that Christ would show to man. These clearly meet the deepest longings of every human heart.

I. **We Need A Savior** (64:1-7)

The New King James Version of the Bible rightly translates verse 5, "We need to be saved." There are four truths that describe the Savior:

1. A Present Savior (vs. 1-2)
In order for man to be saved, God had to come to this earth in the person of Jesus. Indeed, as Sinai once trembled, soon Calvary would tremble at His presence. It is His coming into your life as Lord that saves.

2. A Powerful Savior (vs. 3)
When God comes, awesome things are possible. Who is it that can take a drunkard out of the gutter and put him on a church pew singing Amazing Grace? Who can take the broken remnants of a shattered life and make it useful

219

again? Who is able to turn our midnights of gloom into glory? Only Jesus can do such things. Doctor Jesus never has encountered a hopeless case. Lawyer Jesus has never entered a courtroom and had a client found guilty.

    3.   A Preeminent Savior (vs. 4)

Isaiah rightly describes our God as one who has no rivals. There is no one like Jesus. You can search all of history and you will find Jesus alone at the top.

    4.   A Pardoning Savior (vs. 5-7)

Jesus has come to deal with us at our absolute worst. Our text uses graphic terms to describe the awfulness of sin.

The word "unclean" is the cry of the leper in Israel. Sin divides man from God and from others. The expression "filthy rags" is in the Hebrew *bloody rags* and is the word used for the woman's menstrual flow. Sin defiles the life.

The term "fade as a leaf" means *fading and falling foliage*. Sin destroys and brings death. The sinning life is like a dry leaf cut off from the life of the tree and blown away. The result of sin is a heart dead toward God and a will that refuses to yield. Man has erected a sin barrier between himself and God. Thus God's face is hidden.

II. **We Need A Father** (64:8-65:2)

Fathers are needed for at least three reasons, according to Isaiah. God, as our Father, sets the example.

    1.   Notice His Design (vs. 8).

The image of the *potter* and *clay* describe the relationship between God and His people. Yet He is more than a sculptor, He is our loving Father. He made us what we are.

Jeremiah 18:1-6 says, "The word which came to Jeremiah from the Lord, saying, Arise, and go down to the potter's house, and there I will cause thee to hear my words. Then I went down to the potter's house, and, behold, he wrought a work on the wheels. And the vessel that he made of clay was marred in the hand of the potter: so he made it again another vessel, as seemed good to the potter to make it. Then the word of the Lord came to me, saying, O house of Israel, cannot I do with you as this potter? saith the Lord. Behold, as the clay is in the potter's hand, so are ye in mine hand, O house of Israel."

Children are indeed the product of parenting. God's children are the blessed recipients of His design. He has a plan for our lives.

2. Notice His Discipline (vs. 9-12).

God loves His children enough to discipline them. We need the loving correction of our heavenly Father as described in Hebrews 12:5-11. Here we are told that God corrects all whom He loves and receives. The two-fold result of this divine discipline is: We become partakers of His holiness, and we receive the peaceable fruit of righteousness.

3. Notice His Desire (65:1)

Though the people rebel against Him, our Father is always waiting for us. Notice the double appeal, "here am I, here am I." When the wayward prodigal left home, his father remained right where he left him, at home. Our Father is crying to us through every adverse circumstance, "Here am I." He calls through the noise of everyday life, through the Scriptures, and to our sinning hearts, "Here am I."

Recently, a man asked me, "where is God?" I said, "Friend, God is not lost, you are!" He is standing at the gate of your life and will enter if you will believe. When you see Christ dying on the cross, it is God saying to your guilty soul, here am I! God loves and desires fellowship with us.

III. **We Need A Master** (65:8-25)

Jesus does not come to take a place in your life, He comes to take over. He comes not for a room in your heart but for the keys to every room in your life. He does not come to take a seat in your heart, but to take the throne. He desires to bless us, but we must recognize that He is Master and we are servants. The only way we can expect a blessing from God is to take our place as His servants. Notice three marks of blessing in these verses:

1. The blessing of Home (vs. 8-10)

The promise here is of a place to dwell in this life. The Lord does all that He does for His servant's sake. God has a place of provision for those who live in obedience as servants. If you lack provision it may be that you have missed the will of God.

2.   The blessing of Happiness (vs. 13-14)
These verses declare that the Lord's servants shall eat,
drink, rejoice and sing. *Joy in the Lord* is our heritage.
    3.   The blessing of Hope (vs. 16-25)
These verses speak of a coming day when troubles will be
forgotten (vs. 16). This present world will give way to a new
world. Tears will be gone forever. Prosperity will be the lot
of every person and war and death will be no more.

Conclusion:
    Howard Rutledge, a United States Air Force pilot, was
shot down over North Vietnam during the early stages of
the war. He spent several miserable years in the hands of
his captors before being released at the war's conclusion.
    In his book, *IN THE PRESENCE OF MINE ENEMIES,*
he reflects upon the resources from which he drew in those
arduous days when life seemed so intolerable.
    "During those longer periods of enforced reflection, it
became so much easier to separate the important from the
trivial, the worthwhile from the waste. For example, in the
past, I usually worked or played hard on Sundays and had
no time for church. For years Phyllis (his wife) had encouraged me to join the family at church. She never nagged or
scolded—she just kept hoping. But I was too busy, too
preoccupied, to spend one or two short hours a week
thinking about the really important things.
    Now the sights and sounds and smells of death were all
around me. My hunger for spiritual food soon outdid my
hunger for a steak. Now I wanted to know about that part
of me that will never die. Now I wanted to talk about God
and Christ and the church. But in Heartbreak (the name
POWs gave their prison camp) solitary confinement, there
was no pastor, no Sunday School teacher, no Bible, no
hymnbook, no community of believers to guide and sustain
me. I had neglected the spiritual dimension of my life. It
took prison to show me how empty life is without God."
Only the Lord can fill the deepest longings of our heart.

— ✧ —

Sermon 45

HOW TO HAVE PEACE NOW
Isaiah 66:1-24

Introduction:

In 1989, the world hailed the dawning of peace as the Iron curtain crumbled and communism began to collapse. However by 1991, Russia was facing internal crises so severe that total collapse seemed possible, and the Middle East was poised for war, with Saddam Hussein threatening Israel with the first blow.

Isaiah knew that peace would never come by man's efforts.

I read this story in the newspaper several years ago. Abie Nathan is leading a new children's crusade! Nathan, who operates a pirate radio station aboard his *Peace Ship* in the Mediterranean, has promised to give a scroll with the Biblical quotation from Isaiah, "And they shall not learn war any more," to any child who smashes his military toys. He has also offered to buy the complete stock of war toys from any store which agrees not to sell them in the future.

We admire Nathan's optimism. But there will be no peace on earth, no fulfillment of Isaiah's great prophecy, until the Prince of Peace returns to establish His rule on earth.

How prophetic the words of General Douglas MacArthur, spoken at the end of World War II, sound! At the dramatic moment when World War II ended, General MacArthur spoke the first words of peace to a waiting world:

"Today the guns are silent...the skies no longer rain death...the seas bear only commerce...men everywhere walk upright in the sunlight. The entire world is quietly at peace. A new era is upon us. Even the lesson of victory itself brings with it profound concern both for our future security and the survival of civilization. The destructiveness of the war potential, through progressive advances in scientific discovery, has in fact now reached a point which revises the traditional concept of war... Men since the beginning of time have sought peace, but military alliances, balance of power, and leagues of nations failed, leaving the only path to be by way of the crucible of war.

"We have had our last chance. If we do not now devise some greater and more equitable system, Armageddon will be at our door. The problem is basically theological and involves a spiritual recrudescence and improvement of human character. It must be of the spirit if we are to save the flesh."

Listen to this factual report issued in the last century. On the basis of the computation in the Moscow Gazette, Gustave Valbert in his day could report that "From the year 1496 B.C. to A.D. 1861 in 3358 years there were 227 years of peace and 3130 years of war, or 13 years of war to every year of peace. Within the last three centuries, there have been 286 wars in Europe." He added that "from the year 1500 B.C. to A.D. 1860 more than 8000 treaties of peace, meant to remain in force forever, were concluded. The average time they remained in force was two years."

One of the promises of the Messiah was an age of peace. Man has never been able to accomplish peace on earth. Peace for man and the world is a theme of Isaiah which culminates in our text.

1. In Isaiah 9:6-7, the Messiah is called the "Prince of Peace."

2. This peace is offered on the basis of faith and trust. It is a work done in the heart of man by the power of God. It is experienced by the individual when he receives and recognizes that in Jesus he is righteous.

Isaiah 26:3 says, "Thou wilt keep him in perfect peace, whose mind is stayed on thee: because he trusteth in thee. In Isaiah 26:12 we read, "Lord, thou wilt ordain peace for us: for thou also hast wrought all our works in us. Note Isaiah 27:5, "Or let him take hold of my strength, that he may make peace with me; and he shall make peace with me." Isaiah 32:17 says, "And the work of righteousness shall be peace; and the effect of righteousness, quietness and assurance for ever. (Romans 5:1-5, Philippians 4:6-7)

3. This peace belongs to those who have had their sins forgiven. Sinners can have no lasting peace. Isaiah 57:21 tells us, "There is no peace, saith my God, to the wicked" (Also 48:22). In Isaiah 59:8 we read "The way of peace they know not; and there is no justice in their going: they have made them crooked paths: whosoever goeth therein shall not know peace.

Lastly, notice Isaiah 38:17, "Behold, for peace I had great bitterness: but thou hast in love to my soul delivered it from the pit of corruption: for thou hast cast all my sins behind thy back."

4. This peace was purchased at the cross. Isaiah 53:5 says "But he was wounded for our transgressions, he was bruised for our iniquities: the chastisement of our peace was upon him; and with his stripes we are healed.

5. Peace is maintained by obedience to the Word of God. Isaiah 48:18 tells us "O that thou hadst hearkened to my commandments! then had thy peace been as a river, and thy righteousness as the waves of the sea."

6. Peace with God is lasting and permanent. Isaiah 54:10 states, "For the mountains shall depart, and the hills be removed; but my kindness shall not depart from thee, neither shall the covenant of my peace be removed, saith the Lord that hath mercy on thee."

7. Peace is accompanied by joy. Isaiah 55:12 says, "For ye shall go out with joy, and be led forth with peace: the mountains and the hills shall break forth before you in singing, and all the trees of the field shall clap their hands."

In the Old Testament, peace means prosperity in every realm. Our text is a summation of all of God's promises of peace in Isaiah. In Isaiah 66:12 we read "For thus saith the Lord, Behold, I will extend peace to her like a river, and the glory of the Gentiles like a flowing stream: then shall ye suck, ye shall be borne upon her sides, and be dangled upon her knees."

These final verses of Isaiah hold forth the promise of world peace at the end of this present age. In fact, the final section of Isaiah, 61-66, speaks of events both at the first coming and at the second coming of Jesus Christ. We believe that Jesus Christ's presence means peace to any heart. When He comes, the world can know peace. How can you have peace now in this troubled world?

I. **Make Your Heart His Home** (66:1)

The King of Heaven and earth is looking for a home, a place to rest. When God made the world, He rested on the seventh day. When He comes into a person's life, it is an act of creation (II Corinthians 5:20). After His work of creation, the Lord comes into our lives to rest within us. His presence brings peace to our hearts. You can have peace today by opening your heart to the Lord Jesus Christ. He will place His throne in your heart and take control of your life.

II. **Order Your Life by His Word** (66:2-6)

Notice the phrase, "trembles at my word" found in verses 2 and 5. When we come before the Lord with a broken heart, His Word comforts us. Notice that He promises in verse 5 to appear to us. We are to let His word be our comfort when the world hates us. We are to bring glory unto His name.

III. **Put Your Future in His Hand** (66:7-24)

Many are wondering what the world is coming to. We need not worry for the future is in good hands, the hand's of our Lord. Our text tells us exactly what is going to happen. Follow the theme:

1. Our Lord will "appear" to raise the dead and rapture the believers (vs. 5).

2. His wrath will come on the world in great tribulation. (vs. 6, 15-17).

3. Israel will be restored to her land (vs. 7-11).

4. World peace will come when Jerusalem is secure (vs. 12-14).

5. Nations will be judged on their treatment of Israel (vs. 18-21).

6. God will one day make a new earth and a new heaven (vs. 22).

7. People will either belong to the Lord or spend eternity in hell (vs. 23-24).

Conclusion:

Until the Lord comes back, we can have peace by inviting Him into our hearts. His presence means peace within.

Several years ago a submarine was being tested and had to remain submerged for many hours. When it returned to the harbor, the captain was asked, "How did the terrible storm last night affect you?" The officer looked at him in surprise and exclaimed, "Storm? We didn't even know there was one!" The sub had been so far beneath the surface that it had reached the area known to sailors as "the cushion of the sea." Although the ocean may be whipped into huge waves by high winds, the waters below are never stirred.

The Christian's mind will be protected against the distracting waves of worry if it is resting completely in the good providence of God. There, sheltered by His grace and encouraged by His Holy Spirit, the believer can find the perfect tranquility that only Christ can provide.

— ✧ —